THE ART OF DYNAMIC PREACHING

BOOKS BY PETER-THOMAS ROHRBACH

Non-fiction:

The Art of Dynamic Preaching
Conversation with Christ
A Girl and Her Teens
The Search for St. Thérèse

Fiction:

A Gentle Fury
Bold Encounter

Translation:

The Photo Album of St. Thérèse

PETER-THOMAS ROHRBACH, O.C.D.

The Art of
Dynamic Preaching

A Practical Guide
to Better Preaching

1965

Doubleday & Company, Inc., Garden City, New York

Nihil obstat:	John Clarke, O.C.D.
	Joseph M. Flanery, O.C.D.
	Censores Deputati
Imprimi potest:	Christopher Latimer, O.C.D.
	Provincial
Nihil obstat:	Harry A. Echle
	Censor Librorum
Imprimatur: ✠	Patrick A. O'Boyle
	Archbishop of Washington
	May 18, 1965

Library of Congress Catalog Card Number 65–23781
Copyright © 1965 by Peter-Thomas Rohrbach
All Rights Reserved
Printed in the United States of America
First Edition

This book on preaching is dedicated to my father—
who had to preach many sermons to me.

TABLE OF CONTENTS

"I find the average sermon boring and tedious."

"The sermons in our parish are all the same—as dull as can be."

"The priests in our parish speak poorly—without enthusiasm and, it seems to me, without much preparation."

These are actual statements from average parishioners, people in the pews who listen to our sermons hoping to find in them the words of light and life. The disenchantment reflected in these comments does not, of course, apply to all sermons. Many priests stand up before a congregation, poised and self-confident, and deliver a true message, material that is the product of reflection and consideration, relevant and important to the people, material that is phrased in understandable and contemporary language and communicated with the fire and enthusiasm expected of the man of God. But if the comments of parishioners are true (and the priest is, unfortunately, the last to hear these comments), the forceful and dynamic sermon is more the exception than the rule.

And yet the history of God's Salvation Plan clearly demonstrates the kind of preacher God selected to communicate His reality and His message. The prophets of the Old Testament proclaimed the reality of the living God boldly and bravely, firing their listeners to accept the Lord and do His bidding. They spoke with authority and dynamism, employed sharp imagery, challenged their listeners, inspired them, at times upbraided them—and the people of God *listened*. Elias, Jerimiah, Isaiah: men of God who had a sense of urgency and mission to preach the word of God. This homiletic tradition extended into the New Testament as the apostles and disciples joyfully proclaimed the good news, the ringing truths of Christ's redemption. St. Paul describes this preaching by the word *kerygma*, literally a herald's proclamation of an important truth. The kerygmatic preaching of Paul and Barnabas and Timothy and all those early disciples was a forthright, vigorous, enthusiastic statement of God's revelation, and it established a style and mentality of authentic Christian preaching that should be employed in every epoch of the Church's history. The kerygmatic preachers spoke dynamically and joyfully about God, His love for us, the person of Jesus, the redemption, the paschal victory, grace, sin, the sacraments, the dignity and happiness of the Christian life. They were men who wanted to communicate ideas, and they took advantage of any platform or any gathering to preach the good news. This kind of preaching was the model for so many of the Church's great preachers, for an Augustine and an Ambrose, for a Bernard of Clairvaux and a Bernadine of Sienna, and for all those heralds of the Gospel who could not be contained until they proclaimed the stirring fact of our redemption.

However there has been a discernable decline in the vitality of Catholic preaching since the time of the Council of Trent. In so many instances owlish moralizing and hesitant catechetics have replaced the vigorous kerygmatic preaching of the early Church, and listless pulpit performances, with sermons badly conceived and poorly enunciated have made the sermon something to be endured rather than something to be joyfully received. A cloak of mediocrity descended uncomfortably around preaching as generations of Catholics began to squirm in the pews. Jansenism, too, had its impact on sermons and a blurred image of human nature was presented, and a recurring Pelagianism asserted itself in which the Christian life was described as a mechanical thing measured by inches. But the main problem was the preacher himself: He relegated preaching to a vastly subordinate position in his apostolate, a bothersome chore to be reluctantly performed. Sermons became either perfunctory narrations of catechetical Christianity or verbose harangues full of clichés and platitudes. Priests did not seem to want to take the care and effort to speak well. The dynamic, vital preacher became a rarity. Mediocrity was the order of the day in the pulpit. The fire seemed to have gone out.

But in the 1960's a great moment of Church renewal dawned, and the Catholic community subjected itself to a healthy and searching reappraisal. Mistakes of the past were examined, and remedies of-

fered. Liabilities and weaknesses were assessed. Ineffectual proce-
dures were deplored. The Church set itself to what should be its
continuing obligation: the attempt to make traditional Christianity
relevant and contemporary and effective in every age. Catholic
preaching also came under scrutiny, and a new movement was inaugurated to reaffirm the importance of the preacher's task and to
return to the dynamic, kerygmatic preaching of the early Church.
Pope Paul VI in his *Ecclesiam Suam* stated that preaching is "the
primary apostolate." And the *Constitution on the Liturgy* from Vatican Council II ordered that new attention be given to the homily
which should be preached on every Sunday and holyday. This
preaching should be kerygmatic, the document states. "Its character," the *Constitution* says, "should be that of a proclamation of
God's wonderful works in the history of salvation, the mysteries of
Christ, ever made present and active within us, especially in the
celebration of the liturgy." The document states that we are to
preach Jesus: "His blessed passion, resurrection from the dead, and
glorious ascension whereby 'dying, he destroyed our death and, rising, he restored our life.'" And the material should be gathered from
primary sources: "The sermon, moreover, should draw its content
mainly from scriptural and liturgical sources."

The *Constitution* envisions a dynamic, apostolic preacher, more
prophet than catechist, more herald of the good tidings than dour
moralist. The law of Christian conscience is to be taught, of course,
but in context, in form, as part of the whole revelation of God. "By
means of the homily," the *Constitution* continues, "the mysteries of
the faith and the guiding principles of the Christian life are expounded from the sacred text, during the course of the liturgical
year." We are to announce the loving, acting, paternal God of the
Gospels and St. Paul, not the narrow, mathematical God of the le-
galists, the scribes, the Pharisees. We are to preach the timeless
truths in timely situations, unchanging facts in changing areas,
eternal matters in contemporary sectors, thinking and rethinking
the gospel, making it relevant and challenging in our epoch.

To do this the preacher cannot be a hesitant mouther of platitudes, inarticulate, unsure of himself, unable to communicate and
convince. He must be a herald of Christ—a man with a vital message, who knows how to say it.

This is the preacher's task in our time, this age of renewal.

It is also the reason for this book: to help priests, seminarians, and those interested in good speaking to review (or learn) the basic principles of effective and dynamic preaching, utilizing the best elements in the science of modern public speaking, the timeless *kerygma* of the Church, and the new dimensions of preaching sponsored by Vatican II.

This book is predicated, at the outset, on two fundamental principles:

1. THE AVERAGE PRIEST CAN, WITH ORDINARY EFFORT, BECOME AN EFFECTIVE, DYNAMIC, VITAL PREACHER.

2. IF THE READER OF THIS BOOK FOLLOWS AND PRACTICES THE SIMPLE STEPS OUTLINED HERE HE WILL QUICKLY BECOME THAT KIND OF PREACHER.

These are not casual guarantees wistfully stated; rather, they represent the results and findings of years of working with seminarians in the classroom and priests in the pulpit. These principles work. They work for the average priest (in fact, the author has not encountered a single case where they cannot work), and they can work for you, the reader of this book.

This is a didactic, practical book written with the sole purpose of assisting the reader to become the vital preacher he can become. And while a cursory reading of the book might be helpful in gaining an increased appreciation of the importance of good preaching, the text is arranged for author-reader encounter, with step-by-step exposition and practical exercises for the development of good homiletic technique. It is of enormous importance that the reader employ these few exercises. Only a few minutes a day are required, but these few minutes can make the difference between the mediocre, rather pathetic preacher and the dynamic, forthright speaker the people enjoy. One cannot learn to drive an automobile by merely reading a book about it; practice is necessary. In homiletics, too, practice is necessary, but a directed practice of correct techniques. The old homiletic saw has it: "Practice does not make perfect, it only makes permanent." If one is using improper technique, repeated use of the technique only ingrains it more deeply.

In mentioning technique, we might also state that there is no one single style and manner of preaching that is correct to the exclusion

of all other styles. Good preaching is not that stereotyped a thing:
It admits of many good styles and forms. The science of homiletics
does not attempt to produce a body of preachers who all speak
in the same way and express the same thoughts in the same idiom,
but it does strive to help the individual become his best self,
achieve poise and self-confidence, express important and relevant
ideas, and contact his audience. Two major-league baseball players,
for instance, might use vastly different batting stances, one standing
in front of the batter's box and the other perhaps in the back section
of the box, and yet they could both be successful .300 hitters. Each
player must utilize his own abilities and endowments in the style
that works best for him. Similarly, the preacher must use his own
voice, his own personality, his own mentality, but he must use them
in the best possible manner, getting the most advantage out of
them. Some preachers will speak more quietly than others, some
will be more flamboyant, some more demonstrative, others will mar-
shall their thoughts more carefully and calmly; but they all must
possess that magnetic dynamism of contact and communication,
something so many preachers fail to have. Homiletic vitality, inci-
dentally, does not imply bombast, in the line of the old missionary
axiom, "If you get stuck, shout!" The quiet speaker can be just as
effective as the loud one. The Curé of Ars, Cardinal Newman, Msgr.
Ronald Knox were all soft-spoken men, but they preached with
notable success—because they contacted their audiences, communicated with them, spoke to them and not at them. The task of this
book, then, is not to make you someone else in the pulpit, but rather
to help you become your best self.

The book is divided into three sections:

I THE ART OF PUBLIC SPEAKING
A discussion of the single most important element in preaching: the preacher himself. Exercises in how to gain poise and
self-confidence; how to find your own best voice and project it
to an audience with color and animation and warmth; how to
gesture; how to present yourself to an audience as a vital person with a message.

II THE ART OF PERSUASION
A discussion of the structure of a sermon. How to convince and
persuade an audience; how to make people listen; how to out-

line and construct a sermon; how to give sermons that are interesting and relevant and contemporary.

III   THE ART OF PREACHING

A discussion of the content of a contemporary sermon. The basic message of the good news. How to present the good news in our time; how to use scripture; how to give the Sunday homily. How to preach to special groups: children, teen-agers, missions, retreats.

The material in this book is organized so that the reader can proceed simply and logically through the steps and exercises necessary to develop the effective speaker. Thus we begin with the basic mechanics of good public speaking, for the reason that the preacher must know the dynamics of this particular form of communication before he can hope to project his ideas effectively to an audience. Then, building on this platform, we will proceed to discuss sermon construction and methods for making the sermon material audience-related. Our discussion is pragmatic, not speculative, and we will omit some important material usually considered in discussions of homiletics, such as the moral obligation of preaching, the history of homiletics, the scientific physiology of the human speaking apparatus. As valuable as these matters are, they might overload our text and possibly divert us from our primary objective: to provide a concise, easy-to-follow manual that preachers can use to train themselves to become vital speakers, a manual that contains a clear program for homiletic development that can be studied and quickly reread from time to time as a refresher.

But remember our two promises—and they are personal challenges for you:

You can be a vital preacher!

If you follow the program of this book, you can, with a minimum amount of effort, become a vital, dynamic preacher!

I

THE ART OF PUBLIC SPEAKING

1

THE SPEAKER'S MENTALITY

A number of years ago I had the opportunity of attending a lecture given by an extremely popular preacher. It was an opportunity I had anticipated for some time: The priest had acquired a wide reputation as an effective, interesting preacher, someone well worth hearing. This was a man I wanted to hear, but the occasion had never presented itself. Then I found myself at a convention in Atlantic City and noticed on the program that he was scheduled to give a talk. I joined a group of about five hundred in a large hall, and waited expectantly and enthusiastically for the talk to begin. The priest approached the lectern, acknowledged the introduction, and commenced to speak. My reaction was one of profound disappointment! The man had a relatively poor speaking voice, slightly high-pitched somewhere in the upper registers of the vocal range, and there was nothing extraordinary about his material either, simple, rather ordinary stuff.

I settled back in that vague mood of chagrin one has when something eagerly awaited fails to fulfill its promise. However, when I looked around the hall at the audience I sensed something quite amazing: This man was engaging and captivating his audience; the people were listening to him intently. I studied the speaker anew, this man with the unexceptional voice and material. What did he have that was able to engage this audience so completely? Then I saw it—he had poise. He was relaxed, apparently not nervous, he gestured easily, looked directly at the audience, and he projected, came out at the audience, spoke directly to them. All in all, he gave the impression of a sincere, self-confident man who had something to say to the people and was saying it to them. And, of course, they listened.

This is poise, the essential element of public speaking.

Without poise no public speaker can be truly effective. He cannot command himself, and he cannot command his audience. He will be so ill at ease, even if he manages to camouflage it, that he will erect an impenetrable barrier between speaker and audience. No matter what other quality a preacher may have, no matter how much good will, no matter what message he may have, he will not, if he lacks poise, do his job—he will not communicate with the audience.

Poise, by way of definition for the public speaker, is self-control and confidence, which provide the entire basis for audience contact. It is essentially an interior state of mind that manifests itself in the total deportment of the public speaker as he stands before his audience.

The initial question that the public speaker must decide for himself is whether he is going to take charge of himself and his audience, or whether his audience is going to intimidate and overcome and frighten him to the extent he is ill-at-ease and robbed of his poise. The preacher must say to himself: "Who's in charge here, I or the congregation?" If the answer is "I," then he has poise, but if the answer is "the congregation," he has lost his poise.

The speaker without poise adopts a number of defense mechanisms against the audience that has intimidated and subdued him. He is:

> The shy, diffident speaker who cannot look at his audience, who stumbles and mumbles through his sermon until he has thankfully finished his painful task.

> The panicky speaker who races through his material, short of breath, jamming one word into another.

> The painfully labored speaker who monotonously drones through his material, apparently oblivious to the fact that there is an audience out there listening to him.

> The artificial speaker who employs false inflections and grand Victorian gestures, the kind of speaker that makes a congregation wince because he does not seem interested in communication, only in the pathetic use of a few artless tricks from a bygone era that he uses badly.

And, most commonly, the speaker of some experience who has reached a point of accommodation with his audience: He does not appear to be nervous, and perhaps he is not at this point, but he has been completely intimidated to the extent that he mouths a few clichés and platitudes to the people each Sunday morning, with no apparent preparation, no fire, no dynamism. He mounts the pulpit dutifully, talks in wide circles, sometimes at great length, and eventually drags his talk to a close. He has been thoroughly beaten by audiences, and the tragic part is that many times he does not even realize it.

It is relatively easy to lose one's poise in the arena of public speaking, to become a life-long victim of stage fright in its many manifestations. Public speaking is a special form of communication different than writing or counseling or group discussion or spiritual direction; it has its own rules, its own principles, its own dynamics. Public speaking is a contrived situation where one man must stand before a group and must, by the force of his voice and words and argument, convince his listeners of an idea. This is not a natural, native form of communication, it must be learned. Thus the old Latin axiom has it, *Poeta nascitur, sed orator fit:* The poet is born, but the speaker is made.

The neophyte speaker ascends the pulpit or lectern and looks out at those rows of faces and eyes. They are all looking at him! He opens his mouth to speak, and the only voice heard is his. And when he pauses in his talk, that ominous silence pervades the place and he must rush in with more words to fill the void. The celebrated violinist Fritz Kreisler was visiting the Fulton Fish Market in New York one day, and he paused to inspect a store window that was filled with rows of fish piled on each other, their dead eyes open and staring vacantly out at him. He suddenly turned to his companion, "That reminds me, I almost forgot," he said. "I have a concert tonight." Kreisler's dominant impression of a concert—those rows of *eyes*, open, vacant, staring—can be shared by the public speaker. Eyes! Faces! Ominous silence! It is no wonder he can become unnerved and lose his poise.

However, poise can and must be regained.

Here is the process of losing poise: You are, for example, sitting at a banquet chatting rather pleasantly with your neighbors. It has been a fine meal and you have enjoyed the table discussion. You talked about baseball, a little politics, your trip to Europe last summer. Someone asked you what kind of work you do, and you explained it to the interested attention of your questioner. You even made a few witty remarks that were well received. Then the toastmaster taps you on the shoulder and asks you if you will say a few words to the assembly when the after-dinner speeches begin shortly. Suddenly your mood changes. The pleasant feeling of contentment evaporates. You are going to have to get up on your feet and address all these people. What are you going to say? Well, you can tell them how happy you are to be here and you can wish them all the best of God's blessings. I wish I didn't have to do this, you think. There is an uneasy feeling in your stomach settling uncomfortably over your roast beef dinner. The palms of your hands have become sweaty, and you notice a slight dampness on your forehead. Someone says something to you, but you have to ask him to repeat it. You are involved in your thoughts, thinking about the annoyance of having to address this group.

Then the toastmaster calls on you, and you rise to say a few words. But it is not you, it is only a caricature of you! The charming raconteur of the dinner table has disappeared. The pleasant chap who was able to talk so enthusiastically and interestingly about baseball and Europe, who had such witty things to say, is gone, and in his place is this strained, hesitant, ill-at-ease fellow who speaks in a high-pitched voice and gropes for words.

What has happened? You have been robbed of your poise, divested of your ordinary self-control. *And you did it to yourself!* You talked yourself out of a poised, relaxed frame of mind and allowed yourself to be turned into this dreadful caricature of yourself. Your mental attitude changed, and inevitably you changed. Sitting there at the table waiting to be called upon, you began to think of those rows of faces that would soon be all turned toward you, the eyes that would all be focused on you. In a few minutes, the attention of everyone in this large room would be riveted on you, and you would have to fill this whole room with the sound of your voice. This is where the palms of your hands became a bit moist. You talked yourself out of poise. You lost control of yourself. This other fellow, the other you, took over.

Hence, a principle: *We lose poise in our minds by talking ourselves out of control.*

The dynamics of successful public speaking are relatively simple, but they depend on a solid platform of poise. Let us anticipate our discussion a bit and outline the basic concept of good, contemporary public speaking: something that teachers of elocution are today calling *the Conversational Mode,* a relaxed, natural way of speaking, free of histrionics and dramatics, based on a direct contact with the audience in which the speaker actually talks to the people sincerely and convincingly. In our illustration of the banquet incident above, you talked conversationally to your companions during the course of the meal; but when you rose to address the group, you began to speak artificially, not naturally and conversationally. The dynamics of the Conversational Mode demand that you retain all the naturalness and contact of ordinary human conversation and just project this out to a larger group. Public speaking is good conversation projected. Of course, there are a number of things you have to do concomitantly as you project your conversation: assume greater control of yourself, select your best speaking voice, speak more slowly and distinctly, use greater volume, and project to a larger group. But the core principle of good conversation and public speaking is the same—namely, natural and poised communication between speaker and listener.

Suppose, for example, that you are gathered with a group of three friends describing a journey you have recently made. You are talking effortlessly and animatedly about the things you have seen and the interesting people you have encountered. Your manner is natural, pleasant, conversational. Then another friend joins the group, and then another, and you increase the volume of your voice slightly to include them in the group. Someone across the room hears you speaking and joins his group to your widening circle of listeners. "Let's go over and listen to what Harry is saying," someone else comments. And soon your original group of three has augmented to twenty. As the circle begins to widen you progressively increase your volume, speak a little more distinctly so that all can hear you, become more conscious of the larger audience, and project your thoughts in the same friendly, conversational way to the entire group of twenty. This is a small image of what happens in the Conversational Mode. You retain all the poise of ordinary conversation, all the naturalness, then control it and project it to a larger group —whether it be twenty, or two hundred, or two thousand.

However, this is what so many public speakers fail to do. They

lose all their naturalness in the pulpit. Their native ability to con-
verse, to communicate ideas, which they are doing in hundreds of
private conversations all day long, deserts them as soon as they
stand up before a group of people. They lose control. They become
artificial and wooden. They, in a word, lose their poise.

The unpoised public speaker is similar, for example, to a boy who
returns home after his first trip to the nation's capital. He describes
to his family the adventures of his journey and the historic things
he has seen: the White House, the various monuments, Congress in
session. He is voluble and enthusiastic, and his eyes dance merrily
in his head while he is speaking. His hands flutter excitedly as he
describes the stately buildings in Washington. He is the picture of
animation. Finally his father has to terminate the narrative: "All
right, Joey, tell us the rest of it tomorrow." But tomorrow Joey is in
school, and his teacher asks him to stand in front of the class and
tell about his trip to Washington. Joey rises and begins his narrative,
but it is a different performance from the previous day: He speaks
haltingly and hesitatingly, his arms are rigid at his sides, his eyes
fixed stonily ahead. What has happened to him? He is the same boy
who spoke so vitally to his family, and he is speaking about exactly
the same material. The only thing that has changed in Joey is his
mental attitude. He now has to tell his tale to a group of fifty people instead of the five he was speaking to the previous day. He has
to stand in front of the group and confront all those eyes staring at
him. His natural conversational ability deserts him, and he is a
wooden caricature of himself. Call it what you will—stage fright, the
jitters, self-consciousness—Joey's mental approach to the task of
standing up before the class has destroyed his poise, his ability to
communicate.

A major part of success in public speaking depends on simply
maintaining the naturalness and spontaneity we manifest in our
ordinary conversational habits. But lack of poise prevents this, and
we are unable to do in the pulpit those things we do automatically
in private conversation. And this all happens in our minds. We
talk ourselves out of poise and into a posture of fear and nervousness. If you were to place a plank two feet wide across the center
of a room, you would be able to walk across it indefinitely without
stepping off the board. However, if you were to place that same
board across an open chasm two hundred feet deep, and then make
it as firm as it was on the floor of your room, you would be extremely

loath to walk across it as nonchalantly as you did before. If you did cross it at all, it would probably be on your hands and knees. And yet it is the same board, and you know that you have enough agility to walk across it with no difficulty; but you look down at that drop of two hundred feet and begin to think of the possibility of falling. The more you think about it, the more nervous you get. Your mental attitude robs you of the ability you do possess.

An old homiletic story recounts the fable of the centipede and the grasshopper. One day a grasshopper was bouncing along, and he noticed a centipede crawling on his hundred legs. The grasshopper stopped and stared at him for awhile. Finally he asked: "Say, centipede, how are you able to coordinate those hundred legs and walk without getting your legs all tangled up?" The centipede sat down by the side of the road and studied his legs. "Gosh, I don't know," he said. "I never thought about it." And he remained there, thinking about it, puzzling it over in his mind. The more he thought about it, the more perplexed he became. In fact, he never walked again.

The unpoised public speaker is like that centipede. He thinks himself out of his natural poise. And, in public, he may never talk well again.

If, then, we lose poise by our mental attitude, we must regain it (or retain it) by a reverse process. And this leads us to our second principle: *We regain poise by re-establishing a correct mental attitude, by talking ourselves back into a posture of poise.*

You see a speaker walk to the pulpit. He appears assured and self-confident. He places his hands on the lectern, looks directly at the congregation, and begins to speak. He is relaxed and poised. You think: "He must have ice water in his veins; he isn't even nervous." Not at all! He might be just as nervous as you, but he has controlled it, he has adopted a correct mental attitude to public speaking. The mental acquisition of poise does not mean that you eliminate nervousness completely; it does mean, though, that you control it and subordinate it—and even use it. Nervousness before an audience is quite understandable: It only means that you are alive and reacting. If you had no nervousness, you might be completely apathetic and dull in the pulpit. A nervous, frisky filly can win the Kentucky Derby; but a sluggish, dull one is pulling a cart.

The filly, however, must be saddled and bridled; she must be controlled. The public speaker, similarly, must gain control of himself; he must gain poise. It can be done, and with not too much difficulty either.

It is accomplished, basically, by *thinking* poise. It is life's experience that we become what we think. If you think brave thoughts you will become brave. If you think cheerful thoughts you will become cheerful. If you think depressing thoughts you will become depressed. In public speaking, if you think confidence and poise, if you build the speaker's mentality as we will outline it below, you will become confident and poised.

A soldier in a trench before battle must think brave thoughts, despite his natural nervousness. If he does not, if he allows his fear to intimidate him, he will not be able to charge out of the trench with the vigor and courage necessary for victory.

A baseball player approaching the batter's box at a crucial moment in a game must think confidently to himself: "I can do it. I can meet that ball and drive it for a hit." But if he approaches the plate muttering to himself, "I can't do it, I'm going to strike out," then surely he will strike out.

A golf pro instructing an amateur golfer who is hunched over the ball, lunging at it, will tell him to relax, loosen up, just meet the ball, you can do it. And the duffer does it. He has been instructed in thinking confidence. Mind over matter. Get yourself in control.

It has been said that there are basically two kinds of men in the world: those who walk timidly on the soles of their feet, and those who walk assuredly on the heels of their feet. The diffident ones, and the confident ones. A public speaker must (at least metaphorically) walk on his heels. He must *think* confidence, and then he will *be* confident.

A quarter of a century ago, Dr. Coué popularized in this country his theory of thinking yourself into self-improvement, particularly with his phrase, "Every day in every way I am getting better and better." The Coué school has happily passed from us, but it did contain a fundamental truth: one can think himself into control.

This is the burden of Heywood Broun's classic short story *The Fifty-First Dragon* in which a diffident little fellow is taught a magic word that would enable him to slay dragons. There is no inherent efficacy to the word, of course, but the little man thinks there is and proceeds to slay fifty dragons, muttering the magic word each time. It is only when he discovers the truth that he becomes afraid, and he is consequently slain by the next dragon. When he thought he could slay dragons, he was able to; but when he began to think that he could not do it, then he was not able to do it.

Many elements enhance and develop the public speaker's poise —posture, gestures, voice control—but fundamentally poise is generated in the mind, by thinking poise. The speaker must say to himself, with all determination: *I will be poised.* And he will be.

The validity for thinking poise is built on something we might call The Speaker's Mentality, the frame of mind a speaker must have as he approaches his audience. This is the bedrock for his self-confidence, the reason for his thinking poise. The Speaker's Mentality is composed, for our purposes here, of four attitudes of mind:

1. DESIRE
2. COMMAND
3. COMMUNICATION
4. PREPARATION

These mental attitudes must be adopted by the preacher. His initial task is to think and rethink them until they become part of his mental equipment; then he must continually review them, develop them, intensify them. Without a proper Speaker's Mentality he will be like the little boy recounting his trip before the class, but with a correct Speaker's Mentality he will generate poise and self confidence in himself.

1. DESIRE.

It is an axiom of life that the greater desire and enthusiasm one brings to a task, the greater are his chances of success in it. The young man who really *wants* to be a football player will probably succeed over the man who would merely *like* to be a football player; he will block sharply, tackle vigorously, run swiftly; he will do what must be done because, for some reason, it is personally important to him that he become a football player.

The preacher, too, must have an intense desire to preach well. It must be personally important to him, not as a mere wish but as an urgent imperative within him. If his attitude remains in the area of "I wish I could," he will almost inevitably do a bad job. But if his attitude is one of "I must," then he has taken a giant step along the road to poise.

Desire for anything is developed by the value we place on it.

Accordingly, the priest should possess an urgent desire to preach because of its value and tremendous importance. At the outset, then, the priest should re-evaluate the importance he places on preaching in his ministry; he should attempt to arrive at a practical conviction of why it is personally important for him that he preach well. Briefly, preaching should be important for him:

a. *Because it is important to Jesus.* When Our Lord commissioned the Apostles to continue his work, his fundamental charge to them was: "Go therefore teach all nations, baptizing them in the name of the Father and of the Son and of the Holy Spirit." The first command is to *teach,* and then consequently *baptize.* This, of course, is the proper order of spiritual development: through instruction people are led to the sacraments.

This was the feeling of St. Paul who said: "How shall they believe if they have not heard?" And, in fact, when the early disciples described in the Acts of the Apostles found that their preaching ministry was being infringed upon, they ordained deacons so that they might be more free to preach the word of God. "Woe to me," St. Paul stated, "if I do not preach the gospel." And his strong words to Timothy: "Preach the word, be urgent in season, out of season . . . work as a preacher of the gospel." The *fides ex auditu* (faith depends on hearing) of St. Paul expresses a profound and lasting psychological truth—namely, there is particular efficacy and impact attached to the spoken word which no other form of communication enjoys. Neither the printed word nor any of the many electronic media of communication can equal the results obtained by a "live" speaker. When a man stands before an audience and actually tells them things, the subtle dynamics of interpersonal relationships take over and cause an unparalleled impact. This kind of effect can be obtained through no other medium.

Accordingly, Pope Pius XII called preaching "that primordial instrument of the faith." And St. Pius X in his *Acerbo Nimis* said about the priest's office of preaching: "It is well to emphasize and insist that for a priest there is no duty more grave or obligation more binding than this."

When the priest-to-be kneels in the sanctuary during his ordination, the bishop carefully tells him: "By your preaching may you build the house that is the family of God. The office of the priest is to preach."

On the day of Jesus' ascension into heaven, he commissioned the disciples: "Go into the whole world and preach the gospel to every creature." He makes this same charge to every priest—preach the gospel! It is important to Jesus. It should be important to every priest.

b. *Because it is important to the people.* A current evaluation estimates that in the ordinary American home the television set is played for an average of five hours every day. This statistic has many implications, but for the public speaker today it has one over-riding message: that never before in the history of the world have people been exposed to so much good public speaking. Every ten or fifteen minutes, programs are interrupted by young men with resonant voices and projective personalities who tell us, with *so* much sincerity and conviction, that we have to use this particular tooth paste or drive that particular car. These announcers know the business of public speaking and are intent on getting their message across.

Our average American parishioner might view his television set for two or three hours on a Saturday evening, listening to dynamic announcers persuasively talking about the importance and need of body deodorant, breakfast cereal, and shaving cream. Then a few hours later on Sunday morning he is sitting in church listening to the priest's sermon. And what an unfortunate contrast! The man who is talking about tooth paste is vital, convincing, poised, and prepared. While so often the man who is talking about the most important news in the world, God's revelation to mankind, is flat, dull, hesitant, diffident, disorganized.

By comparison, the priest fares badly, and the emotional reaction of the parishioner is hard to deny: that, somehow, tooth paste seems more important to the TV announcer than God's message does to the priest. The parishioner who is eagerly waiting for some message from the priest is profoundly disappointed; and the parishioner who listens to sermons apathetically, in a "show me" attitude, remains apathetic and returns home unconvinced and unchanged. The priest has done poorly by his people. They deserve better than that. Our people are conditioned to good public speaking today, and they expect it from the priest. And if they do not get it, they will not listen.

Another fact of modern living: Although in America today we are in the possession of more labor-saving devices than any time in our history, we seem to have gained little time at all; in fact, we appear to have less time at our disposal for things we would really like to do. We are rushed, harried, busy, always moving at a pace that is just this side of the frantic. We save a little time by the use of electric dishwashers and electric clotheswashers (even electric toothbrushes and shoeshiners!), but then we squander it on bowling and cookouts and interminable cocktail parties and the hundreds of other events which seem so necessary in the Affluent Society. As the pace of life keeps quickening, we never seem to find time for so many important things.

Religion suffers here, and people donate less time to things of the spirit. In former eras, the Christian people built their lives around the church. They attended Mass on Sunday morning and returned again in the afternoon for Vesper services; they frequented evening services; and they participated in the Christian festivals, celebrating them as holidays with liturgical services and processions. But all that has changed, and the only enduring thing that remains is attendance at Sunday Mass. As one old pastor put it: "In the old days, all I had to do was put on the lights, and the church was filled. Today you have to raffle off a Cadillac to make them come."

The point of relevance is: The sermon at the Sunday Mass is the only consistent and enduring occasion when we can communicate the message of God to the Christian people.

We might dismiss that statement and produce a number of statistics to attempt to shout it down, but we are deluding ourselves. Can we reach the people through the printed word? A few of them. A book of Catholic persuasion is considered a substantial success if ten thousand copies are purchased. Estimating that each purchased volume is read by four or five people, it only means that a successful book is read by fifty thousand people out of a total Catholic population of nearly forty-six million people. A negligible amount, one tenth of one percent. Catholic newpapers remain largely unread; they are often purchased because of diocesan loyalty, hastily perused at best, and quickly thrown with the day's outgoing pile of newspapers. And what about special parish organizations? If a group of two hundred people attend a sodality or society meeting, we might consider that satisfactory attendance; but the particular parish might have four thousand people in it, and the group represents only a minor fraction of the parish. The church is almost half-filled for novena services some nights. Fine! But on Sunday morning thaht same church is completely filled seven times.

Apart from the Sunday Mass, we are encountering only small fractions of the body Catholic. Granted they may be important, key fractions, they are still not the body Catholic.

The priest, therefore, has a unique and unparalleled opportunity each time he ascends the pulpit on Sunday. He is presented with the challenge and the privilege of encountering the Christian people and communicating the message of God. But if he wastes the opportunity, it can be compensated for in no other area.

A consideration of this situation should enhance the priest's desire to address the congregation. The sermon should be regarded not as a *chore,* but as an *opportunity.* The ancient joke about the advertising executive who offered the Pope five million dollars if he would have priests at Mass say "Drink Coca-Cola" instead of "*Dominus vobiscum*" contains a kernel of intriguing truth: the Sunday Mass congregation is a fantastic audience to address. How many men with something to say or sell would pay a small fortune to address this congregation? And yet this opportunity belongs to the priest each Sunday, and so often he squanders it. "Woe to me if I do not preach the gospel."

To recapitulate: The priest will speak more dynamically, with more poise, if he has an urgent desire to preach. And this desire is germinated and augmented by a personal conviction that preaching is important. Important to Jesus, who commissions his priests to preach. Important to the people, who are conditioned to good speaking today, who need the message of God they can receive nowhere else.

2. COMMAND.

When a teacher walks into a classroom at the beginning of a term there ensues a subtle but definite contest, a struggle for control. Will the teacher take command of the children, directing them to increased learning and fulfillment? Or will the children dominate the teacher, ultimately reducing the class to a shambles? Something of the same situation prevails when the preacher ascends the pulpit. Will he take charge of the audience, or will they take charge of him?

"Who's in charge here?" That is the initial question the priest must answer.

If the priest is in charge he will stand up and speak forthrightly and authoritatively, with conviction and assurance and poise. But if he allows the audience to take charge of him, he will be quickly intimidated, nervous, hesitant, unsure of himself.

Assuming command of an audience does not imply hauteur or arrogance or a mood of "jam it down their throats." The priest is not to take charge in the posture of a top sergeant, but rather as an instructor who knows his material and is here to tell it to the people. He is the "boss" of the moment, who kindly but firmly communicates his message to the audience.

An attitude of command can only initially be created in the speaker's mind. Therefore, the priest has to convince himself of three realities:

a. You *are* a priest, and this is your job. You are appearing in the pulpit in role. You are not here auditioning for the job, begging for a hearing. You have been commissioned by Christ to preach, to take charge of this audience. And take charge you will!

b. The congregation *expects* you to take charge. Your business is to preach to them, and they are waiting for you to do it. The people are well-disposed toward you; they are friendly. Many of them might be apathetic and somewhat indifferent, but they are not hostile. "You are the priest," they say. "Preach to us." In fact, they are embarrassed when you fail to take charge, when you appear frightened and nervous and hesitant. They expect and want you to be the "boss" of the moment.

c. You are a professional in the matter of religion and you should know your business. The Catholic laity is a more highly educated group today than at any time in American history, and we must accordingly prepare our material better and speak more intelligently, but still the average layman is not a professional theologian. You have taken a long seminary course, spending four years of post-college study in scientific theology; you have been thinking and reading and praying about these matters for years. You undoubtedly know more about religion than anybody in the average audience. This does not mean that you should speak down to your audience, but it should give you enough confidence to take charge of your audience and talk about those things in which you are a professional. Furthermore, no one in *any* audience knows your sermon today: it is *your* message and you know more about it than anyone else.

These are the three attitudes which should generate a "take charge" mentality in the preacher. He has everything in his favor, even the physical arrangements: the audience is seated and the preacher is standing, the best possible arrangement for an attitude of command.

Answer the question for yourself, then: "Who's in charge here?"

3. COMMUNICATION.

Public speaking is, as we have stated, conversation projected. Thus both public speaking and good conversation must share that same fundamental quality: communication. We do meet people in life who are poor communicators—the person who averts his eyes when we talk to him, who says "Yup" and "Nope" when we ask him a question, who appears uncomfortable in our presence, who seems to want to get away as soon as possible. To such a person we might say: "Be more direct with people, stick out your hand and shake hands enthusiastically, look people in the eye, appear interested in them and not yourself, develop your personality."

A similar situation exists in the area of public speaking: Some priests are poor public communicators—they do not look at the audience, they speak haltingly, appear uneasy, and seem more concerned with their own discomfiture than the interests of the congregation. And to him we would also say: "Be more direct with your audience, establish eye contact with the people, become interested in them, develop your speech personality."

The priest must not only take charge of his audience, he must also communicate with it. There must be a speaker-listener encounter in which the priest speaks *to* the people and not *at* them. The mood of communication manifests itself in many of the physical aspects of the speaker's presence—in his forthright manner, his firm voice, his eye contact—but it is primarily generated in his mind, in his mental attitude. These are the steps for developing an attitude of communication:

a. *Create an urgent desire to communicate.* The desire to preach, founded on our efforts to please Jesus and the needs of the people, must be further constructed into a desire to communicate. The priest must not merely *appear* in the pulpit; he must use the pulpit as a launching pad for audience contact. He does not merely *recite* a sermon; he *tells* his message to the people. Convinced of the necessity of preaching, the priest now needs to think in terms of a live audience, people waiting to hear his words. And he should want to talk to them, communicate with them, tell them things. Preaching is an experience of real personal encounter, and the priest must reach out to the people. He has burning, important, critical things to say; and he must have an irrepressible urgency to say them.

The listening congregation is not a herd, a faceless group, a composite of eyes and ears and faces and overcoats and ladies' hats. It is a gathering of many individual people, and each person has his own life, his own history, his own aspirations, his own fears, his own achievements. You, the preacher, must speak to every one of these people. You are not standing on a mountaintop making a pronouncement for the ages, you are in this church speaking to these two or three or four hundred people. They are looking up at you, waiting to hear you; and you must speak to *them*.

In the sacristy before a sermon, the priest could profitably say to himself: "I've got something to say, and I'm going out there and speak to these people, tell them things." Then his mood will be projective, audience-directed.

b. *Develop your speech personality.* A speech personality is an attitude of immediacy of contact between speaker and audience, one of rapport and rapprochement. It is best developed by creating a *private* speech personality that can be employed and used in your *public* speech personality: that is, by using projective techniques in your daily meetings with people so that you can carry these habits into the pulpit.

In the example cited above of the poor communicator, we encourage him to be more direct with people, look them in the eye, shake hands firmly. That is the method of developing your private speech personality. Whenever you meet someone and shake his hand warmly and look him directly in the eye as you are speaking to him, you are developing your speech personality and your poise. But whenever you are shy and diffident, whenever you cannot think of anything to say, whenever you avert your eyes in embarrassment from someone while talking, you are constructing bad habits of personal encounter and further destroying your poise.

In the pulpit you have to *force attention,* and you can practice this in your private dealings with people. Walk up to someone, speak directly and enthusiastically to him, and get him to listen to what you are saying, do not let his attention escape—in a word, force attention. It might mean overcoming native shyness or embarrassment, but if you are determined enough you can get someone to listen to you. Then your increased facility at forcing attention should be applied in the pulpit: When you are standing before a congregation you should employ the same determination to capture their attention.

If you are a person who walks up to a friend and says, "Harry, uh . . . I . . . uh . . . want to . . . ah . . . tell you . . . something," then try forcing Harry's attention next time. Walk up to him directly and say crisply, "Harry, I want to tell you something!" And do the same thing (figuratively) in the pulpit: say crisply, "People, I want to tell you something." And do not let them escape until you have told it to them.

The next time you meet a stranger, say to yourself the two key words *force attention,* and then proceed to do it. It is invaluable practice for the public speaker: It develops your projective technique and engenders an attitude of self-confidence and poise which you should retain when you ascend the pulpit.

c. *Confront the audience.* The preacher must confront the audience and force attention. Confrontation, then, should be the public speaker's mood. He has to be aggressive and forthright, and not allow the audience to slip away from him. Confrontation is a mental attitude but it works hand and glove with three physical elements:

i. *Eyes.* The preacher must look at his audience. Many speakers avert their eyes, look down at the lectern, gaze at the lighting fixtures, study their hands—anything to prevent an eye confrontation with the audience. The net result, of course, is that the audience does not respond, does not listen as attentively; because people almost instinctively mistrust, or at least suspend assent from someone who will not do them the courtesy of looking at them while speaking.

It is a relatively simple thing to look directly at the audience during a sermon—if only the preacher makes up his mind to do it. Once the preacher has forced himself into it, a habit is formed, a habit of eye contact; but if the opposite habit is formed, a preacher could spend a whole lifetime nervously looking away from the people, never really confronting his audience. A speaker should continue shifting his gaze during the course of the entire sermon so that he encompasses the entire audience, looking now at the people on his right, then his left, those in the front, those in the rear. Not, however, in a manner that is so stylized and mechanical that the audience is conscious of a planned pattern (one-two-three, *shift,* one-two-three, *shift*) but gracefully, naturally rotating his gaze to bring everyone under the influence of this homiletic experience.

If a speaker is unduly nervous at the beginning of a sermon, fearfully intimidated by all the eyes staring at him, he could direct his gaze over the heads of the congregation, fastening it on a spot halfway up the rear wall. This gives him the appearance of looking at the audience. But as soon as he adjusts himself, he should bring the direction of his gaze back to the audience and look at the people he is addressing.

The mature personality has no difficulty looking directly at a person while engaging in conversation. The priest should, by all means, have enough maturity to confront an audience with his eyes.

ii. *Breathing.* Proper breathing is important for the public speaker because breath is the fuel for our talking machine. We will discuss this more fully in its proper place, but there is one element of breathing that is helpful for confrontation: breathing as an antidote for nervousness.

You have perhaps noticed how a professional athlete employs breathing to calm himself in a moment of tension. For example, the baseball pitcher who finds the bases loaded, no out, and the brunt of the batting order coming to face him, will often do something suggested by his coaches: pause and take deep, long breaths. This serves to steady him and stifle his nervousness.

Public speakers often employ this technique of deep breathing to rid themselves of the jitters, and the priest could profit from their experience. In the sacristy before a sermon, the priest could take three or four long, deep breaths, filling his lungs with air and slowly exhaling; he will find that it has a calming effect, giving him greater control of himself. Or in the pulpit, in those few moments when the congregation is settling back in its seats, the priest could breathe deeply and silently before starting his talk. A few deep, controlled breaths can assist the priest immensely in his confrontation of the audience.

iii. *Posture.* Good platform posture is similarly something that we must examine more fully at a later point in our discussion, but one element is extremely important in generating poise: that is, the attempt to give physical expression to the mental attitude of "walking on your heels."

The priest who walks to the pulpit, places his hands firmly on the lectern, squares his shoulders, and looks out to the congregation, presents an immediate picture of poise, relaxing the people and inviting their attention. But the priest who shuffles his feet in the pulpit, clutches his hands tightly in front of himself, and peers over the edge of the lectern like a soldier in a trench looking out at the enemy, presents an immediate picture of uncertainty and confusion that unsettles the audience and makes it more difficult for them to believe what this man is saying.

Thus the priest in the pulpit should be conscious of his posture. He should plant his feet firmly on the ground. He should square his shoulders naturally and easily. He should consciously do something with his hands so that they appear controlled. One excellent technique for initial pulpit posture is to grasp the two sides of the lectern with your hands in the manner in which you hold the steering wheel of a car. Driving instructors sometimes suggest that the novice driver hold the wheel at "ten minutes to four," the left hand higher on the left edge of the wheel and the right lower on its side. That is a good position for the speaker's hands at the beginning of a talk: the left hand high on the left edge of the lectern, the right hand lower on the right side. It is a traditional public speaking posture, one that presents an instant image of poise, and it can be employed as a starting posture to steady the speaker at the beginning of a sermon.

It might be well for the public speaker in the privacy of his own room to study his public-speaking image in a wall mirror. Does he appear poised, relaxed? Does he look audience related, direct, immediate? Or does he have the "rabbit image" in the pulpit, someone who seems to have been propped up there and is staring helplessly out at this group of people confronting him? This is not to suggest that public speaking is artificial pose or posturing—quite to the contrary. But the preacher's inner poise should reflect itself in his general deportment and composure in the pulpit. A survey in front of a mirror can provide an appraisal of this.

Squared shoulders, hands firmly on the pulpit, direct eye confrontation of the audience—these present an immediate image of poise. And, by a process of reciprocity, they make the preacher *feel* more poised. He feels like a man who is walking on the heels of his feet.

To recapitulate: Communication, that attitude of speaking directly and immediately *to* the audience, is generated by creating an urgent desire to communicate, by developing one's speech personality, and by confronting the congregation.

4. PREPARATION.

An essential element in the development of poise is preparedness on the part of the speaker. Nothing unnerves the speaker as much as lack of preparation, and nothing else can generate the kind of confidence a speaker has when he knows what he is going to say. In part two, the Art of Persuasion, we will discuss the mechanics of preparation, but our point now is that preparation is an absolute necessity, an essential prerequisite for poise.

Unfortunately, too many priests deliver what has been called "the steer's-head sermon"—a point here and a point there, and a lot of bull in between. The congregation recognizes this type of sermon immediately and reacts to it with profound disappointment and disapproval. Here is a man standing before them in the pulpit, fumbling for ideas, searching for words, punctuating his performance with tired platitudes, gyrating uncomfortably until he mercifully drags his remarks to a close. Hardly a poised, direct speaker.

On the other hand, a priest who works on his sermon, who marshalls his thoughts, perhaps does some research, organizes his material, makes a full outline of his sermon, will almost certainly enter the pulpit with greater poise and self-confidence. He will have the assurance that he knows what he is going to say, and there is no way of gaining that assurance except through preparation.

Preparation does not imply the composition of a full manuscript and a memorized, word-for-word presentation of it. The most serviceable and practical method, as we will describe it later, is the construction of a full, detailed outline, and then a direct presentation based on the outline. The memorized recitation can be too stiff and consequently destroy the excitement and immediacy of audience contact. The type of outline we are discussing, of course, is not merely a few phrases scribbled on the back of an envelope, but a carefully planned, well-organized arrangement of ideas. This demands time and preparation.

Nor can the preacher escape the demands of preparation by carrying his manuscript or a sheaf of notes into the pulpit with him. A sermon is direct, person-to-person communication between preacher and audience, and a manuscript or notes destroys this relationship by forcing the speaker back into his notes. As the bon

mot has it: "Using a manuscript while making a speech is like court-
ing a girl through a picket fence—every word can be heard, but
there is not much contact." Despite the fact that a preacher might
forget an idea or a phrase by not using notes, this is more than compensated by the electricity of communication. A sermon given from
notes is almost invariably flat and dull: the preacher is using a
crutch and therefore cannot be completely poised.

Regarding preparation, the rule is simple: Take the time and
effort to prepare your sermon well! If you do not, if you merely stir
together a few platitudes for the congregation, then you almost
automatically place yourself in an unpoised position. And the audience detects it immediately.

The "steer's-head sermon" is a disservice—both to the preacher
himself, and to his audience.

Desire. Command. Communication. Preparation. These are the
elements of poise, the material out of which a mental attitude is
constructed. The veteran speaker, as well as the neophyte, must
think these things through, making them a basic part of his mental
equipment. And having learned them, the speaker must return to
them frequently, rehearsing them in his mind, strengthening his
attitude of poise. Poise is a growing, developing thing; it must be
nurtured and cultured until a man can stand before an audience in
a mood of self-confidence and control, until he is able to recover
enough of his native naturalness to communicate effectively with
the people.

Other factors are extremely important in the creation of an effective speaker—the proper use of the voice and the selection of
pertinent material, for example—but they will be of small help if
the speaker does not build on a platform of poise, if he does not
construct a proper speaker's mentality.

Control! This is a concept we will return to frequently in our
discussion. The speaker needs control—control of himself, control of
his audience, control of his material. When the preacher steps into
the pulpit, the lights playing on him and the audience staring at
him, he is in a pressure situation. He can easily allow the tensions
of the moment to overcome him and thereby lose control. It is here
that his speaker's mentality must sustain him and carry him through
so that he can do his job. The literary generation of the 20's coined

a phrase that has application to the speaker's problem: "grace under pressure," the ability to remain calm and poised in situations of great stress and tension—either in individual situations or in the large business of living itself. The classic demonstration of grace under pressure was performed by the matador in the bull ring. Alone, armed only with a cape and sword, the matador stands in the ring confronting the onrushing bull. He must swirl his cape and draw the bull back and forth across the ring, allowing the animal to pass inches from him, and he must not panic nor lose his poise. He must be relaxed, graceful, in control of himself. Grace under pressure.

This is not to suggest that the preacher in the pulpit is a Hemingwayesque figure, alone, abandoned, facing hostile forces. Quite to the contrary. The preacher is facing a friendly audience that is sympathetic to him, eager for his success. But nevertheless it is a "moment of truth," a tense situation demanding grace under pressure. The preacher, like the matador, cannot afford to panic. He must be relaxed, graceful, in control of himself. He must be poised.

And to accomplish that, he needs to construct a speaker's mentality.

EXERCISES

- Ask yourself some searching, personal questions:
  - In the area of public speaking, am I poised, relaxed, self-confident?
  - Or am I strained, artificial, intimidated by the audience?
  - Do I know how to gain poise?

- Review the nature of poise:
  - You lose it, like the centipede, by talking yourself out of it.
  - You regain it by a reverse process of talking yourself back into it.

- Review the elements of the speaker's mentality:
  - Desire:
    - The more enthusiasm you have for preaching, the more poise you will possess, and you should want to preach—a) because it is important to the Lord, and b) because it is important to the people.
  - Command:
    - You should develop a "take charge" attitude because a)

this is your role as preacher, b) the congregation expects it, and c) you are a professional speaking about your business. Ask yourself: Who's in charge here?

- Communication:
  - The preacher must communicate with his listeners, talk *to* them. To accomplish this you must a) create an urgent need to communicate, b) develop your speech personality, and c) confront the audience by eyes, breathing, posture.

  (Practice communication by "forcing attention" in private conversation. Learn eye confrontation. Do deep breathing to lessen nervousness. Study your platform posture before a mirror. Begin to walk on the heels of your feet.)
- Preparation:
  - Make a firm resolution to prepare your sermons.
  - Take the pledge to avoid the steer's-head sermon.

- Restudy these principles of poise frequently until they become a basic part of your mental equipment, until you can maintain grace under pressure.

2

YOUR BEST VOICE

The speaker's voice is the medium of contact between the preacher and the audience. The ideas in his mind are communicated to the minds of the congregation through the means of his voice. It is, therefore, a fundamental item in the preaching experience.

Public speakers frequently make two common mistakes in the use of their voice: they do not use their best voices; and they do not control their voices.

Everyone has a different voice, but everyone has his own *best* voice. The speaker who is indistinct, who slurs words, who is shrill or high-pitched, who jams words together, who speaks in a flat monotone, is not using his best voice. This is highly detrimental to the effectiveness of preaching. First of all, if the audience cannot hear or understand the speaker, the sermon is a complete failure. But, equally important, the listening audience reacts to the voice of the speaker and adopts an attitude toward what the speaker is saying on the basis of his voice. We tend to do this in our daily encounters with people. If a person speaks too rapidly with a high-pitched voice, we immediately form the impression of a rather callow, immature person, pleasant enough but not to be taken too seriously. The fellow with the gruff, deeply guttural voice is thought to be tough, insensitive to our needs, somewhat unapproachable. One who speaks with a weak, hesitant voice is judged to be unsure of himself, someone in whom we could not place much confidence. These judgments are sometimes unjust and incorrect, but we do make them, almost unconsciously. Try this experiment sometime: Close your eyes and listen to the people speaking on television without looking at them, and you will find that you tend to make judgments about the people you cannot see on the basis of their voices.

The congregation, similarly, adopts an attitude toward the preacher on the sheer basis of his voice. If the priest is using his voice improperly he could very well communicate an unfortunate impression which would affect the success of the message he is trying to communicate. But if a preacher uses a firm, distinct voice, if he modulates and colors it, if he projects warmly at the people, then the audience settles back to listen. This is a man who is poised and sure of himself, the listener seems to say, I want to hear him. The priest should want to communicate that kind of image.

Control of one's speaking voice is also vitally important. Some speakers are at the mercy of their own voices. They merely open their mouths and listen to what happens. The speaking mechanism is a human function and should be controlled and directed, just as the athlete controls and directs the use of his arms and legs.

The speaker who does not have conscious control of his voice, who merely listens to himself speak, is forfeiting an opportunity of inestimable value. He cannot use his voice as an instrument, an agent for communication. If a man has control of his voice, he can use it in a variety of different ways to give more meaning to what he says: he can modulate it, shade it, regulate the volume, emphasize certain points more forcefully. In other words, it is *his* voice, and he can use it to do what he wants.

The purpose of this section is to provide a succinct and popular outline of the speaking mechanism so the preacher can understand his own voice, use it, and control it. Our explanation is pragmatic and descriptive, rather than scientific and physiological; designed to provide the preacher with a working description of his own voice. Then we will give four rules that the speaker can use and practice to gain mastery of his voice.

The physical aspects of the human voice can entail a long and detailed study because the mechanism is complex and composed of many parts. However, we shall keep our outline brief and simple, make our rules few and pointed. That is all the journeyman preacher needs to know for effective preaching. Mastery over one's voice can be accomplished by a relatively easy process—if the speaker follows these few steps.

THE SPEAKING MECHANISM

In simple outline, the speaking mechanism is composed of three principal parts: motor, vibrator, and resonator.

It is extremely valuable for the public speaker to know the elementary functions of these parts so that he may more effectively use the instrument of his voice. A simple method for understanding the nature and function of these parts is a comprehension of the fact that the human voice is fundamentally a wind instrument and shares basic similarities with many musical wind instruments. The clarinet serves as a fine example. It, like the human voice, has three parts: motor, vibrator, and resonator. The motor is the mouthpiece into which air is pumped. The vibrator is the long middle section, the tube through which the air passes and vibrates so that it makes a sound. The resonator is the horn at the end of the instrument, the small, tulip-shaped device which magnifies sound.

Motor, vibrator, resonator—these produce the musical sound in the clarinet. The motor, the mouthpiece, pushes the air. The vibrator, the long reed, oscillates the air so that it causes a low sound. The resonator, the small horn, magnifies the sound and gives it color. The human voice is produced in the same general way, and the clarinet can help us understand the process.

Make a mental image of a clarinet and place it upright against the figure of a man. Hold it upside down, so that the mouthpiece is at the man's belt and the horn near his lips. The two sound producing mechanisms are now in parallel position.

The clarinet's motor, the mouthpiece, is opposite the man's speaking motor—his abdominal muscles and lungs. The clarinet's vibrator, the reed, is opposite the man's speaking vibrator—his larynx, the vocal cords in his throat. The clarinet's resonator is opposite the man's speaking resonator—his mouth and nasal cavities.

The human clarinet, if you will, then produces sound in the same manner as its musical counterpart. The motor (the abdomen and lungs) pushes the air upward. The vibrator (the vocal cords) vibrate under the pressure of the pushed air causing a low sound. The resonator (the mouth and nasal cavities) picks up the sound, magnifies it and gives it color.

Let us take a closer look at the three parts of the speaking mechanism so we can understand their function.

Motor. Air, as we have stated, is the fuel of the talking machine. It is drawn into the body through either the nose or mouth. Then it is pulled down into his chest cavity (thorax) and his lungs until it strikes a sheet of muscle called the diaphragm. The diaphragm, a vital organ in proper speech, is a sheet of muscle and tendinous fiber, dome-shaped in its relaxed state, that separates the cavities of the chest and the abdomen. In proper breathing, the air is pulled in deeply enough so that it fills the entire chest cavity and pushes the diaphragm into a flattened, level position. Then the motor begins to operate correctly: the air is pushed up from the diaphragm and lungs.

Vibrator. The air, which has been compressed in the lungs and then released, now passes into the larynx, the membranous tube at the Adam's apple sometimes called "the voice box" or vocal cords. This tube is composed of a number of heavy, triangular membranes and muscles. When the air passes over these membranes and muscles they begin to vibrate and produce a sound, in much the same manner as the strings of a harp vibrate and produce a sound when they are plucked. The sound produced by the vocal cords themselves, however, is thin and weak.

Resonator. The sound from the vocal cords passes into the chambers of the nasal passages and the mouth where it is amplified and made rich and colorful. The nasal chambers give richness and resonance to the sound arriving from the vibrator; while the mouth gives distinctness and force.

The human voice, then, in summary: the air is forced up from the diaphragm and lungs; it passes over the vocal cords in the throat, causing them to vibrate and produce a sound; the sound is resonated in the head, then moulded and shaped and forced out through the mouth.

We are now ready for four practical rules that will enable us to use the speaking mechanism properly.

1. MOTOR CONTROL.

Many speakers do not use their vocal motor in the correct manner. In fact, in the area of the proper use of voice it is the fault most frequently committed, and the one that is most infrequently recognized.

Proper use of voice demands that the public speaker draw his breath deeply enough into the chest cavity so that the diaphragm becomes flattened. If this is done the speaker can reserve enough air for the amount needed in public speaking, and the air itself is pushed upward with greater force and control.

This type of breathing, which speakers (and singers) must employ, is called "diaphragmatic breathing" or "abdominal breathing" or "medial breathing." It requires that the speaker use his abdominal muscles when he breathes, pulling these muscles in so that the air is drawn deeply down into the chest cavity.

Preachers frequently breathe only from the upper portions of the chest so that they puff the air in and out of their lungs, rather than drawing it deeply into the entire cavity and thus allowing it to flow out smoothly and strongly. Abdominal breathing is the natural and easy form of breathing, and when we are most relaxed it is the form of breathing we employ. If you observe a man sleeping on his back you will notice that his stomach rides up and down as he breathes— abdominal breathing! The preacher has to get those belt muscles moving when he is speaking in public, pulling them in so that he can draw in a full supply of air. If he does not, his air supply is greatly diminished, and he is using what has been called "pinched air."

The speaker must pull his diaphragm into a flat, level position when he breathes, but the diaphragm is one of those muscles about which we have no sense of position. We cannot directly feel it, nor directly and consciously control it. For this reason we control it and pull it out of its conical shape into a flat position by using the abdominal or belt muscles. Every time you take a deep breath, sucking in the air from the abdomen, pulling in your stomach, you automatically flatten the diaphragm.

The first function of proper voice control, therefore, is correct speaker's breathing. The speaker, of course, must breathe through his mouth while speaking, and he must condition himself to short but powerful breaths. He should not become so preoccupied with the business of making sound that he forgets to draw in sufficient air, nor should he breathe with only the upper portion of the chest cavity. He needs to train himself in the use of his belt muscles, pulling his stomach in as he breathes and then allowing it to expand naturally. He must "breathe from the stomach." Then his voice will be firm and well-supported.

Hence, the first rule: *Stand erect and breathe from your stomach, pulling in the abdominal muscles while you speak.*

2. VIBRATOR CONTROL.

The vocal cords in the throat vibrate under the pressure of the air which is being forced upward. Like the strings of a harp, they must be taut, but they must not be so tight that they emit a harsh, tinny sound. If the strings of the harp are too tight, they give a strident, metallic sound, but if they are moderately taut they give a pleasant colorful sound.

The speaker's task, therefore, is to keep his vocal cords relaxed. The more tense the cords become, the more unpleasant a sound is produced—either harsh, or rasping, or shrill, or hoarse, or brassy. The average male vocal cords vibrate at a frequency of 124 double vibrations per second (B on the scale), while the female vocal cords, which are strung in a more tense position, vibrate at a frequency of 244 double vibrations per second (b on the scale). Thus the tighter the tension, the faster the vibrations, and the higher the note.

One specific "warm up" exercise is quite valuable for relaxing the preacher's vocal cords, either as immediate preparation for a sermon or as a program exercise for developing relaxation in the throat. In this exercise, imagine that your head is attached to your shoulders merely by means of one cord; then let it fall forward on your chest and start to rotate it slowly toward your right shoulder, then over the shoulder and allow it to hang down toward your back, and finally draw it over your left shoulder and bring it back to its position on your chest. Repeat this slow rotary motion a number of times, rotating your head in circles to the right and in circles to the left, keeping your throat as loose and relaxed as possible. You will find that the tension will drain out of your throat and it will become loose and relaxed—perfect position for the vocal cords during public speaking.

To maintain this posture of relaxation during speaking, the preacher should straighten his shoulders, drawing them slightly back, not in a position that is stiff but in one that is firm and comfortable. We tend to allow our shoulders to slouch forward and this inhibits the relaxation of the vocal cords. The speaker could imagine that he has a coat hanger placed in his coat and he must comfortably square his shoulders to prevent discomfiture.

Squaring one's shoulders during public speaking accomplishes three values: 1) it prevents the hunch and slouch of the shoulders which tighten toward the neck, tensing the vocal cords; 2) it spreads the chest, allowing for more air intake; 3) it gives you more of a feeling of control, of walking on the heels of your feet.

Our second rule: *Square your shoulders, drawing them comfortably back into a posture of relaxation and control.*

3. RESONATOR CONTROL.

a. *Nasal Resonance.* The sound produced by the vocal cords must be augmented and magnified; otherwise, it would not be audible for more than a few feet. This augmentation is accomplished principally in the nasal cavities, although some slight contribution is made in the upper throat. The process is called resonance and is similar to a procedure occasionally employed by recording artists in cutting musical records: they "chamber" the voice by standing in a small enclosure when they sing, and as the voice rebounds off the chamber overtones are caused and the voice itself sounds more resonant and colorful.

The speaker has the benefit of his own private "chamber," the nasal passages, which resonate and augment and color the voice. Some speakers, however, do not take advantage of the chamber and do not resonate their voices properly.

Resonance is the hum in a person's voice, and is chiefly used for the *m* and *n* sounds and the vowels. Good spoken English demands that these sounds be resonated. You can test for resonance by huming *m* and pinching your nose: you should be able to feel a sensation of vibration in your nose if you are resonating properly.

The resonant quality in the human voice, therefore, is produced in the nasal cavities behind the mouth and nose, and the speaker must make a conscious effort to "push" his voice through this area. He must, in the parlance of public speaking, speak through the mask of his face, that general area that would be covered by a small *mardi gras* face mask: the eyes, the nose, the upper lips. The sound must be pushed out through this mask; that is, the speaker needs to direct and project the sound through this area.

This is the correct way to project sound. However, if the sound is not projected correctly it will be projected in other directions with unfortunate results. There are three incorrect directions for the voice to flow: 1) it can be projected off the upper section of the head, and it then will be high pitched; 2) it can be projected through the front of the face, either the end of the nose or the teeth, and it will be either nasal or indistinct; 3) it can be projected through the throat, and it will be muffled and guttural. (Nasality, therefore, derives not from too much use of the nasal cavities, but from too little: nasality is caused by speaking from the tip of the nose.)

The preacher's task, then, is to project his voice neither from the top of his head, nor the front of his face, nor his throat, but through the mask of his face. He must make a mental image of the point from which his voice should emanate—above the upper teeth, at a focal point back of his nose. From this point, he must push his voice out. Then his voice will have color and timbre; it will be warm and human.

An old public-speaking exercise is helpful in finding and maintaining your proper resonance sound. Recite the sounds: MO-OH-EE-OH-AH. Say them slowly, drag them out. Now hum them, attempting to make them as resonant and as colorful as possible. In the "nose-pinch test" your nostrils should be vibrating. Practice this exercise frequently, using it as a means to discover your resonance point of sound projection, and as a warm up exercise prior to public speaking.

The third rule: *Project the sound of your voice through the mask of your face, selecting a point of projection above the upper teeth and behind the nose.*

b. *The Articulators.* The final step in the proper production of voice is accomplished in the mouth and teeth. If the sound is projected through the nasal cavities, through the mask of the face, it is given precision and distinctness in the mouth and teeth, the articulators. While the *m* and *n* and vowel sounds are created in the nasal resonator, the hard consonants are enunciated in the articulators.

English is a language that is heavy with hard consonants, and if they are not bitten off sharply and distinctly the sound will be slurred and muffled. Lip laziness is an all-American vice, and when Method Actors attempt to portray American speech they often mumble their words. But this will not do for the public speaker: he must be heard.

This final step in the proper use of voice demands that the teeth and lips be used effectively—the teeth must *bite;* and the lips must *move.*

In their natural position the lips lie in a horizontal position, but in public speaking they must be operated in a more oval, rounded position. As a warmup, the preacher could moisten his lips, then run his tongue around the outside of his mouth, stretching it as far as it will go—not a very dignified posture, but one that makes the lips more mobile and flexible for enunciation.

The public speaker has his own problem of "DT's," the clear and distinct enunciation of the *d* and *t* sounds. If they are not carefully pronounced they will be lost to the audience completely, and the result will be an indistinct speaker. They are two of the more difficult hard consonants, and the preacher can use them as a test of clarity, asking himself the question: Can my DT's be heard?

As an exercise, try talking through clenched teeth in the manner of the movie gangsters of the 30's and ascertain whether you can pronounce the DT's in this posture. With clenched teeth, say the words *ended, identity, fender, titanic.*

The recitation of tongue twisters is excellent practice for the public speaker, and we will cite a number of these in the exercise section at the end of this chapter. An accomplished recitation of tongue twisters is not merely a feat of virtuosity; it gives the speaker control of his voice and mastery of the hard sounds he must make.

Physiologically, the vowel sound of the human voice is magnified in the nasal resonators, and the hard consonants are enunciated in the tongue-teeth-lip area. But as a practical rule of thumb for the speaker, he should concentrate on our rule: Project the sound through the mask of the face, and bite off the sound with the lips and teeth. Then he will be producing sound correctly and effectively. As a test, say the phrase *Father Manning,* and pinch your nostrils while saying it: you should feel vibration on the word *Manning* and no vibration on the word *Father.* This is the proper balance between resonance and articulation.

The fourth rule: *Bite the projected sound with lips and teeth to give sharpness and precision.*

SUMMARY.

The adoption of these four rules, then, will enable the preacher to discover his own best voice and master it for the purposes of public speaking.

Abdomen pulled in, drawing air down to the diaphragm. Shoulders spread comfortably apart, allowing the throat to relax. Sound projected through the mask of the face, from a point above the upper teeth and behind the nose. Words bitten off sharply by the mouth and teeth to give distinctness and precision and sharpness.

As a mnemonic device, the four rules can be compressed into ASRM—for Abdomen, Shoulders, Resonators, Mouth: the four areas of concentration for the public speaker in the control of his voice.

Accordingly, we shall refer to these four rules of voice as "the ASRM principle."

The four rules must be employed simultaneously and in coordination. They are designed for control of the entire speaking mechanism, from origin to final delivery, and proper use of voice demands mastery of the entire procedure. While each of the four rules of the ASRM principle can be practiced separately, the goal should be a coordination of the process to give one total effect. It is similar to learning how to drive an automobile: There are a number of different elements to learn—steering, braking, use of rear mirror—and each one must be mastered, but finally they must be coordinated into one performance. The novice driver has difficulty in coordinating these skills, and he must give conscious and deliberate effort to the procedure; but after practice, he is able to drive and coordinate these skills as almost an unconscious habit. The preacher, similarly, will grow in mastery of the four rules, and they will constitute his habitual manner of speaking.

Practice, however, is essential for mastery of the four rules. A mere reading of the principles and a desire to employ them are not enough. There must be a program of practice, not sporadic but regulated, day after day until the ASRM principle becomes a part of the speaker's spontaneous performance. If the reader of this book would donate three minutes a day to practicing some of the exercises at the end of this chapter, he would in six months radically change his platform presentation. Practice in anything is of enduring value only when the practice is consistent and programmed. A few minutes a day of practice is enormously more valuable than an entire hour now and another hour sometime a few weeks later.

The preacher could make no resolution quite as profitable as the one to practice the ASRM principle for three minutes a day over a period of six months. It will repay him staggering dividends.

Remember: It is your voice—and you must discover the best voice you have, and then master it!

EXERCISES

Memorize the four rules:

1. Stand erect and breathe from your stomach, pulling in the abdominal muscles while you speak.
2. Square your shoulders, drawing them comfortably back into a posture of relaxation and control.

3. Project the sound of your voice through the mask of your face, selecting a point of projection above the upper teeth and behind the nose.

4. Bite the projected sound with lips and teeth to give sharpness and precision.

Daily exercises for practicing the ASRM principle:

Rule 1: Take ten deep breaths with your mouth, drawing the air deeply in to your stomach, so that your abdomen goes in and out.

Pull your stomach tightly in, as tightly as possible so that you seem to be pushing it up against the backbone; and hold it there for six seconds, with your mouth open. (This is an "isometric exercise." It will not only reduce the size of your waist; but, as a value for the speaker, it will give you control of those belt muscles we so seldom use.)

Rule 2: Rotate your head around on your shoulders, allowing it to fall free and relaxed.

Square your shoulders comfortably, imagining that you have a coat hanger still in your coat and you must adjust your posture so that it can remain there comfortably.

Now study yourself in a mirror to ascertain if your stomach is in and your shoulders spread. Keep relaxed, and take some more deep, diaphragmatic breaths.

Rule 3: Find your resonance projection point—above the upper teeth and behind the nose. Pull in your stomach and hum the letter m, holding it and directing it out through the mask of the face. Make sure that you are not humming through the top of your head, or in your throat or through your nose.

Recite MO-OH-EE-OH-AH. Hold the last AH, and hum it. Repeat this five times, with stomach in and the lips free and flexible.

Rule 4: Moisten your lips. Pucker them and relax them a number of times to make them more flexible and mobile. Move your tongue in a rotary motion outside your lips, stretching it as far as it will go.

Recite distinctly the words: ships, casks, masks, tasks, nests, gusts, mists, pests. Make certain that the final *s* is heard.

Recite that immortal piece of doggerel: Theophilus Thistle, the successful thistle sifter, thrust three thousand thistles through the thick of his thumb, and the reason that Theophilus Thistle was such a successful thistle sifter was that he was able to thrust three thousand thistles through the thick of his thumb.

Recite: Brittle bricks bother big bridge builders.

Recite: Slippery sleds slide smoothly down the sluiceway.

And: Sister Susie's sewing shirts for soldiers.

Recite three times rapidly: Lemon liniment.

Recite this old English teaser: She stood at the door of Burgess's fish-sauce shop welcoming him in.

Recite this limerick:

> There was a young person named Tate
> Who went out to dine at 8:8
> It is sad to relate
> What a person named Tate
> And his tête-à-tête ate at 8:8.

Recite the above tongue twisters a number of times, coordinating the entire speaking procedure so that stomach is in, shoulders spread, sound pushed through the face's mask. Say them with clarity and precision and distinctness, biting them off carefully so that *you* are in command of your speaking mechanism.

Review the principles of chapter one, The Speaker's Mentality, and coordinate this with the ASRM principle. Stand before a mirror, strike a posture of poise, and recite one of the tongue twisters, using your voice properly.

3

THE CONVERSATIONAL MODE

Good contemporary public speaking is conversation projected. That implies that the public speaker address his audience naturally and sincerely, free of artificiality and pose. The era of high-blown oratory has fortunately passed into history, that time of artificial orotund tones and sweeping dramatic gestures, that epoch in which the shout was more important than the idea. Today effective speakers attempt to communicate with their audiences as warm and sincere human beings, employing all the direct techniques we use in ordinary conversation. And the ultimate impact is one person *talking to* other people.

In the example cited in chapter one, we posed a situation in which one person is talking with a small circle of friends, effortlessly and with animation. Then he is joined by a few more friends, and then a few more, until the circle widens to include twenty people. As the group increases, the speaker begins to speak with greater volume, pronounces words a little more distinctly so that he can be heard, becomes conscious of the larger group, and projects his remarks to twenty people instead of the original three or four. But in this relaxed atmosphere the speaker retains all his naturalness and poise, all his sense of person-to-person communication, all the cadences of natural voice inflection. He is simply projecting his conversation to a larger group of people.

This, in miniature, is what the Conversational Mode demands. The speaker must retain all the techniques of good conversation, and then adapt them to a larger audience. He must speak naturally, gesture naturally, employ natural voice cadence; but he also must pace himself more carefully, speak more loudly, and project to a large audience. We will examine these elements of the Conversational Mode in this chapter under the headings of:

1. MODULATION
2. VARIETY
3. PACE
4. GESTURES
5. PROJECTION

1. MODULATION.

Modulation is the first and basic element of natural, conversational speaking. It is fundamentally a combination of pitch and emphasis which produces the cadences of expressive human speech.

Were you to chart the pitch and emphasis rate of a person talking in an ordinary situation, you would have a graph of irregular jagged lines, rising and falling in peaks of different lengths. This is the ordinary manner of human speech. The average person emphasizes different words within the same sentence at varying degrees of emphasis, and he pronounces words and phrases at different levels of pitch. The preacher must bring these same cadences into the pulpit with him, employing all the expression and inflection of natural speaking.

So often, however, the preacher freezes in the pulpit, and what is produced is not natural human speech but a false and artificial sound. Speech defects in this area usually fall into one of two categories: the monotone and the singsong.

It is almost impossible to speak in a true monotone, maintaining the level of pitch on one true note, but some speakers come fairly close to it. They open their mouths and merely emit the sound, straight, uninflected, and colorless. This is the same kind of sound made by the train announcer in the railroad station—"The Afternoon Congressional for Washington, D.C., is ready on track nine; dining car and coaches to the rear, parlor cars to the front. All aboard, please." We listen to that kind of speaking, not because it is an experience of deep human communication, but only because we urgently need the information.

The singsong cadence is the nervous little inflection adopted by the speaker who has been intimidated by his audience. He artificially limits the vast range of the human voice to a guarded little one-two routine. This is the sound made by the small boy standing before his class, arms riveted to his sides, reciting a memorized

poem—"The boy stood on the burning deck, da-*da*, da-*da*, da-*da*."
We only listen to that kind of performance when we have to, and
there is no escape.

The preacher, having established a speaker's mentality and having gained mastery of the speaking mechanism, must immediately
proceed to an examination of his modulation techniques. Am I, he
must ask himself, speaking with natural modulation? Or am I,
perhaps, speaking in a monotone? Or in a singsong pattern?

He needs to recall that human speech is modulated; it rises and
falls in natural cadences. For example, the sentence, "That is precisely the point!" might be said in this pitch arrangement:

```
                    ly'
              cise-
         pre-           the
     That is            point!
```

Or the sentence, "Do you really believe that?" in this manner:

```
                         that?
         Do you      believe
              rea-
                 ly
```

There are other ways of enunciating these two sentences, and the
various nuances of pitch and emphasis we might employ would
change the meaning slightly. And that is the purpose of modulation:
to emphasize what we say, to add color and meaning to our words.

Here is a vignette, a dialogue between husband and wife at a
party. The words in italics are inflected words, emphasized as they
would be in normal speech patterns. Try reading the scene in a
monotone with no particular inflection, and then read it again stressing the italicized words. You will notice immediately the difference
between normal, meaningful speech and colorless, artificial recitation.

The Guests

HE: Are you ready to go *yet*?
SHE: *I'm* ready, but are *you*?
HE: I've been *ready* for half an hour.
SHE: What's the *big rush* to get home?
HE: I'm afraid it's going to *snow*.

SHE: I looked at the forecast before we came—it said *no* snow.

HE: Well, look out the window, will you? It's *snowing now*.

SHE: It wasn't *supposed* to.

HE: *Supposed* to or *not*—it *is* snowing. Let's get going, *please*.

SHE: Don't get *nasty* now.

HE: I'm not *nasty*.

SHE: You're certainly not *friendly*.

HE: I'm not *nasty*, I'm not *friendly*, I'm not *anything*. I'm just afraid of that *snow*. You don't want to spend the night here at the *Smith's*, do you?

SHE: You make a *point*.

HE: Thank *God* for small favors.

SHE: Now *don't—*

HE: *All right, all right*. I'm sorry. Just get your *coat* on.

The natural effect of modulation can also be demonstrated by the use of one word. Take the proper name "Harry," and say it a number of different ways and you will see the different meanings you can bestow on it. For example:

HARRY (Question: Is that you, Harry?)

HARRY (Imperative: Stop that, Harry!)

HARRY (Disgust: Harry, you broke my razor again.)

HARRY (Amusement: Harry, you're a card.)

HARRY (Request for attention: Harry, let me explain it to you.)

HARRY (Admiration: Harry, you're the greatest.)

HARRY (Contempt: That old crazy Harry.)

HARRY (Love: Harry, I love you.)

Or use a simple, apparently declarative word like "yes" and observe how many different meanings can be attributed to it by various vocal inflections:

YES (Emphatic: Yes, sir!)

YES (Evasive: Maybe yes and maybe no.)

YES (Enthusiastic: Oh, yes, it's wonderful.)

YES (Sarcastic: Oh, yes, you're always right.)

YES (Boredom: Yes, dear, I'm listening to every word you say.)

YES (Annoyance: Yes, what do you want now?)

YES (Suspense: Yes, doctor, what's the diagnosis?)

YES (Ecstatic: Yes, Clarence, I'll marry you.)

As an exercise, the public speaker can use a simple declarative sentence, and discover how many different meanings he can contrive by inflecting different words. For example, use the sentence: *John gave the hat to Mary.* Then, reciting the exact same sentence, answer these questions by changing inflection:

> Who gave the hat to Mary? (Stress *John*)
> To whom did John give the hat? (Stress *Mary*)
> What did John give to Mary? (Stress *hat*)
> What did John do? (Stress *gave*)

These are exercises designed to alert the preacher to the naturalness of modulation and to remind him that he does modulate in his ordinary conversations without reflection or necessity of practice. The problem is that frequently the public speaker becomes so unnerved by the entire experience of appearing in public that he transmutes himself unwittingly into an artificial caricature of himself, a wooden shell emitting expressionless and uninflected sounds. This kind of speaker, therefore, needs to work on his modulation. And this does not imply instruction in some new art he must study and learn; it merely demands that he retain in the pulpit all the expression and natural inflection he employs in his other vocal uses. This can be accomplished in three steps:

1. A searching personal appraisal of whether you are speaking with natural inflection or whether you have driven yourself into a position of poor modulation. A voice recording on tape would be helpful, as would be the candid opinion of some listener. But you can also learn a great deal about your own pulpit performance by listening to other preachers as they operate in the pulpit. Observe their modulation techniques and note whether they are employing natural inflection. Ask yourself, when you witness a pulpit performance: Does this man speak with expression and modulation? Or is he speaking in a flat monotone? And then: How do I compare with him? Do I modulate naturally as this man does? Or perhaps do I speak in a flat monotone as the other man does? A great deal of insight into one's own performance can be gained from observing another man's performance and then making an honest comparison.

Parenthetically, we might note that the preacher should make it a general rule for himself to listen to as much preaching as possible. The more preaching we hear, the more we learn about it. But the preacher must listen to other sermons and speeches with the ear of a professional. It has been said that a football coach watching a game on television does not watch the game in the same manner as an ordinary fan: He is a professional, and he observes the professional techniques of the game—how the team is coached, what general kinds of offense and defense the coach has plotted, what specific moves the players have been trained to make. The preacher, similarly, is a professional in his business, and he must listen to a sermon from this posture. He must note the vocal techniques of the preacher, his audience contact, his ideas and his method of presenting them to the congregation. He can learn much from the effective things he watches other preachers do, telling himself, "There's a technique I should use," or "There's an idea I might incorporate into one of my sermons." But, since we are such peculiar things, we human beings, we learn more from others' mistakes than their accomplishments; and accordingly, we can profit by observing the things other preachers do badly, telling ourselves, "There's a vocal mistake I'm making, too," or "His ideas are muddled, I must be careful to be more clear than he is." The professional always welcomes the opportunity to watch other professionals at work, and the priest should bring a serious, professional attitude to his function of preacher.

2. Modulation is acquired, secondly, by reviewing the principles of poise outlined in the first chapter of this book. Poise gives the speaker a platform of naturalness, and modulation is basically the projection of natural speech patterns. Thus, the more poise the speaker possesses, the better he will modulate. The preacher needs to remind himself that he is speaking *to* the people, not merely enunciating words and sentences before a large audience. Preaching is a form of human communication, a person-to-person contact in which the preacher expresses ideas in a human and natural manner. But he must relax, maintain control of himself in the pulpit, because if he loses his poise there is great danger he will become so stiff and taut that his voice will come out expressionless and uninflected.

3. Finally, the public speaker can practice modulation techniques by reading aloud to himself from some book. As he reads, he

should make a *conscious effort* to modulate, to employ the ordinary techniques he uses in daily conversation.

Since modulation is a natural rhythm in the speaking process, it would be tedious and harmful to chart specific points of pitch or emphasis in the printed text he is reading. He should simply remind himself of the necessity of speaking with expression and inflection, and then follow the natural course of his relaxed speaking delivery. It is similar to the situation in the classroom when the teacher of early grade students tells one of her pupils, "Now read with *expression*, Johnny!" The public speaker, in the practice exercise, must tell himself: Read with expression!

If the speaker is relaxed and natural enough in this exercise he will notice his voice rising and falling in natural cadences. However, at the beginning he might have to force modulation a bit to inaugurate the process, pushing his voice down at certain points of emphasis and elevating it at others. This is excellent, because it gets the process moving. One caution, though: the cadences should be natural and meaningful. Here are two test sentences, with the points of inflection italicized:

> He is peculiar, but I *like* strange people.
> He who is not with me is *against* me.

In the first sentence *like* should be inflected upward; and in the second sentence *against* should be inflected downward. This is the meaningful way to modulate the sentences.

A few minutes a day of reading aloud, coupled with a conscious effort to modulate, can produce a marked improvement in a speaker's natural speech patterns.

Appraisal. Poise. Modulation practice. These are the steps to better modulation technique. Modulation, it should be noted, is not dramatics or histrionics; there is nothing artificial about it. Quite to the contrary. It is natural and human, emanating from within the man and giving meaningfulness to what he says and thereby making his message more understandable.

2. VOCAL VARIETY.

In addition to the basic voice cadences we call modulation, the human voice has other dimensions of expression that are employed occasionally to add greater impact to what we say. A man speaking in an ordinary conversation will modulate his voice naturally, inflecting it expressively, but he also has enough control of his speaking mechanism that he can vary the rate of speed at which he speaks, change the volume, pause, drive home a point more forcefully. He does this almost unconsciously, and it adds variety to his presentation.

The conversational mode, a human, natural way of speaking, demands that the speaker bring into the pulpit all of these natural expressive techniques he employs in private conversation. They add variety and naturalness to his pulpit performance. We will consider them under four headings:

> a. Rate of Speed
> b. Volume
> c. Force
> d. Pause

a. *Rate of Speed.* If you listen to someone speaking in a private conversation, you will notice that he varies the rate of speed at which he is speaking during the conversation. He will say some things more slowly and deliberately, other things more rapidly and perfunctorily. If he is describing, for example, a trip to Hawaii he might recount the details of his air trip at a more rapid rate of speed ("We took off from Los Angeles at nine o'clock and flew out over the Pacific at an altitude of thirty thousand feet."), but when he describes his first view of Hawaii he reduces the rate of speed, speaks more slowly, and expresses the wonder of it all ("There we stepped out of the plane into the gleaming sunlight, and it was magnificent!"). This is a natural and almost unconscious speech pattern.

The public speaker should similarly vary his rate of speed while speaking, saying some things more rapidly, other things more slowly. Otherwise his rate becomes monotonous and uninteresting.

The accomplished public speaker talks at a rate of somewhere between 120 and 160 words a minute. (The neophyte often speaks at a much more rapid rate, and we will consider this problem when we discuss *Pace* shortly.) But working from his basic rate of speed, he can accelerate or decelerate to give greater meaning to what he is saying. If he is talking about something momentous and important, he will speak at a slower rate; but if he is speaking of matters of secondary importance or filling in some details, he will speak a little more rapidly.

A preacher, for example, might be relating the events of the Last Supper, speaking a little more rapidly as he recounts the details of the seating arrangements, the Apostles, the bread and wine; but when he begins to describe the institution of the Eucharist he speaks more slowly.

As a practice exercise, the preacher might read aloud the entire account of the Last Supper, varying the rate of speed at different sections. If, however, he discovers he is speaking at the identical rate of speed during the whole reading, he should recognize that his rate is too monotonous and not quite vital enough.

Since the more common American speech fault is too rapid a speaking rate, the point of concern for the preacher should be his ability to slow down, to emphasize more important points by a slower rate of speed. If he is able to do this, if he is able to express more important truths by a deliberate, slower rate of speaking, he can feel confident that he is employing a basic technique of the natural conversational mode.

b. *Volume.* The "shout and holler" school has happily departed from the mainstream of American homiletics. Nevertheless, the preacher should be able to vary the volume within his sermon so that he can contribute added emphasis to what he is saying.

Manipulation of volume is, once again, a basic technique we employ in ordinary speech patterns. A mother speaking to her child will enunciate this sentence at a medium level of volume: "Billy, what did you learn in school today?" But she will undoubtedly elevate the volume for this sentence: "Billy, I don't want you to leave the house this afternoon."

The preacher should be able to employ the same techniques, elevating and lowering the volume to emphasize points. For example, recite the following sentence:

> Jesus Christ is the son of God; and Philip is one of his disciples.

Recite the first part of the sentence at greater volume, and then recite the second part following the semicolon at a lower volume. Notice the greater impact added to the sentence. Or use this sentence, changing the volume at the semicolon again:

> The kingdom of heaven suffers violence; and the violent shall bear it away.

The preacher can manipulate the volume, speaking either more loudly or more softly to gain a variety of different effects. Recite the following sentence, and raise the volume at the italicized words:

> Christ promised to remain with us to the end of the world, and *he is faithful to his promise.*

And now the following sentence, softly lowering the volume at the italicized words:

> Christ established the Virgin Mary as the mother of all mankind, and *she loves us with a mother's heart.*

Volume control, speaking more softly or more loudly at different times within the sermon, is one more form of vocal variety. It adds more meaning and naturalness to what we say.

c. *Force.* A preacher, as we have mentioned, must force attention, get the audience to listen to him. This is a general attitude during a sermon, but there are specific instances in the sermon itself when the preacher wants to add greater emphasis, to grab them by the lapels as he drives home his critical points. We call this technique *force.*

This is the same technique we employ in conversation when we say something like this: "Listen, buster, I'm telling you for the last time: get out of my house and stay out!"

Force, which is basically strong emphasis, is created by two elements previously discussed: volume and speed. Hence, a principle: *to gain the greatest amount of force, slow down and say it more loudly.*

Recite the following sentence, applying force at the italics (i.e. slow and loud):

> They say that Christ is just a good man, but I tell you *he is the living son of God.*

You obtain more impact that way, than by merely running the sentence along at an even rate.

Or use Churchill's famous statement:

> We will *never* surrender.

The force word is *never,* and the full meaning would be lost by rolling over it.

Here is an excerpt from a sermon by the popular Redemptorist preacher, Father Joseph Manton. The force words are italicized. Read it aloud, force the italicized words (loud and slow), and you will see how much vitality and dynamism you can add to his remarks:

> Whoever claimed sanctity was sending your fingers galloping round and round a rosary like a runner doing his laps round a track? Or that holiness consisted in lighting a lot of vigil lights like a pious pyromaniac, a kind of theological arson? Or attending three different novenas a week like a juggler keeping three colored balls in the air at once? . . . Men and women have become saints without any of these, *but nobody ever became a saint without saying or at least meaning many times the hardest little sentence in the English language: Thy will be done.*

Force is one of the most useful techniques a speaker can master. It is relatively simple to employ, takes a minimal amount of practice, and can add a whole new vitality and intensity to the speaker's message. It is, of course, an occasional device to be used sparingly and judiciously during a sermon, but if a preacher really wants to drive home a point, let him say it *slowly* and *loudly.*

d. *Pause.* A pause during conversation is usually a command for attention. The person who says, "George, I want to ask you something," and then pauses, is issuing a command for attention. The person who states, "I want to tell about the three most fascinating women in my life," and then pauses, is drawing our attention closer to his remarks. And the preacher who employs a pause carefully in his sermons can summon greater attention.

Pause is difficult for the neophyte preacher to employ because he feels a compulsion to rush on and fill the empty void of silence created when his words cease. Another difficulty is that the pause always seems longer to the speaker than it does to the audience. But if the preacher can gain enough control of himself he can use this effective technique of human communication in the larger area of public speaking.

A pause at the very beginning of a sermon, before the preacher actually begins to speak, is quite valuable for drawing the audience's attention to the speaker. As the congregation settle back into their seats, there is always a slight bit of shuffling and restlessness;

the preacher should pause and remain silent until the people quiet themselves and their attention becomes drawn to the pulpit. This is the "pregnant pause," full of expectation of interesting things to come. When the speaker has thus pulled the congregation's attention to himself for five or ten seconds, he can begin crisply and sharply, knowing that he has maximum attention.

An intelligently employed pause within the sermon itself can add greater emphasis to what the preacher is saying. He may use it either before an important idea or immediately after it. For example, the preacher might state in the course of his sermon, "I want to ask you a vitally important question this morning," and then pause and hold it a few seconds; he will automatically summon greater attention to what he is going to say. Or he might state, "One day, at an hour and a date as yet unknown, you are going to die and stand before Christ, the judge of all people," and then pause, allowing the idea to gain greater impact in the minds of his listeners. The pause thus employed becomes a vocal means for underscoring key ideas.

If a sermon ends sharply enough, the conclusion can be driven home with particular force by pausing for a few seconds and sustaining the mood before the speaker leaves the pulpit. One of the most effective sermons I ever heard on the issue of civil rights was given by a young priest who spoke about the issue obliquely, emphasizing Christ's command to love all people. He concluded his sermon by painting the scene of the crucifixion and describing the horror and the dirt and the gore, and then he said:

> As you recall that scene and reflect that in the moment of Jesus' agony almost all His friends deserted Him, you might say to yourself 'If only I had been there, I would not have deserted Him, I would not have run away from Him.' But if you are not able to see Christ in the person of the Negro, I wonder if you would have been able to see God in the person of that dirty, bleeding figure on the cross that Good Friday. I wonder. (*Pause*) I wonder. (*Pause*)

The two pauses at the conclusion of this sermon had an electrifying effect on the congregation and said more than an hour of thumping oratory.

The oratorical pause is the device that requires the least amount of practice, for all it demands is that the speaker say absolutely nothing for a few seconds, but it is nevertheless one of the most difficult techniques for the novice speaker to master. The beginner is always afraid of that ominous silence when his voice stops and he needs self-mastery to sustain a pause. But it is worth the effort. The pause can create what is called in public speaking "a magic moment," one of those rare moments in the course of a talk when the attention of every listener is riveted on the speaker, when you can hear the proverbial pin drop. Any experienced speaker knows that those moments are rare indeed in any talk, but they can be induced through the judicious employment of the pause.

The Conversational Mode is predicated on naturalness, and therefore very few of its elements can be rehearsed or deliberately planned during the composition of a talk. The pause, however, is one of the few exceptions, particularly for the beginner. The preacher could profitably plan an occasional pause at a key point in his sermon: the necessary pause, of course, at the beginning of the sermon that summons the attention of the audience to the speaker; the pause before a pivotal idea, or before a question is addressed to the audience, or after an incisive point has been made. Try it. The pause will help you to create a "magic moment."

In summary, vocal variety can be added to your sermon in four ways: rate of speed, force, volume, and pause. These techniques bestow naturalness on your performance and make you appear more human in the pulpit.

3. PACE.

To return to our original analogy about the Conversational Mode: You are speaking casually to a small group, then as more people join the group you extend your remarks to the larger audience while retaining all of your naturalness. One fundamental thing that you must do in this experience is speak more slowly and slightly more deliberately so that the entire group can hear your voice. This basic requirement of the Conversational Mode is called *Pace,* the tempo at which the public speaker should talk to be properly heard.

Successful public speaking demands that the speaker talk at a slower rate of speed than is usually employed in ordinary conversation. Otherwise his speech will not be distinct enough for the audience to follow. Excessive rapidity of speech is another All-American speech fault, and the contemporary public speaker must check himself on this when he ascends the platform.

The accomplished public speaker, as we have noted, talks at an average rate of somewhere between 120 and 160 words a minute. This seems to be a fairly adequate rate, allowing the audience to hear comfortably and the speaker to sustain the dynamism and vigor necessary for the Conversational Mode. As a preliminary test exercise, the speaker could time himself as he reads aloud from some passage and then count the number of words he has read in a three-minute period. If he finds that he is in great excess or defect of the 120- to 160-word margin, he will know that he is speaking either too deliberately or, more commonly, too quickly.

The way to halt excessive speed in public speaking and sustain a proper tempo is by inserting *vocal commas* in your speech. A vocal comma is a slight pause during the spoken word that serves the same purpose as the printed comma in the written word: it separates ideas and thus phrases the sentence properly. The pause of the vocal comma is different from the oratorical pause we discussed in the preceding section: that pause of three or four seconds duration is inserted to summon attention, while the vocal comma is a split second pause used to break the sentence into phrases. It gives the speaker "holding power" over his words, enabling him to harness the rapid speed he tends to employ, particularly when he is nervous.

Listen to a news commentator on radio or television and note the way he employs the vocal comma to create greater distinctness and clarity. Here is a Reuters Dispatch phrased as a radio announcer might read it. Read it aloud, with a vocal comma, a slight pause, at the phrase marks:

> Sydney / Australia. / The Dutch freighter Van Cloon / today took in tow / the U.S.-bound Swedish freighter Lake Ontario, / which was disabled after being swept by fire / 250 miles from New Caldonia in the South Pacific.

> The Lake Ontario / will be towed 900 miles to Sydney. / Most of its crew were taken on board a French ship, / the Polynésie. / None of the Lake Ontario's crew / was reported injured.

The preacher in the pulpit will not, of course, speak quite as deliberately as that, but he should employ the technique of the vocal comma to maintain a pleasant, understandable tempo. This demands practice *before* he ascends the pulpit, and the most serviceable practice is reading aloud with proper attention to phrasing.

Reciting poetry is particularly beneficial (the iambic pentameter of Shakespeare, for example) because some basic kind of phrasing is absolutely necessary to give intelligibility to it. Or the preacher could annotate some pages from any book with phrase marks as we did in the Reuters Dispatch above, and read the passages aloud. Here is the Gospel for the Fourteenth Sunday after Pentecost (Luke 17, 11–19) thus annotated:

> At that time / on his journey to Jerusalem, / Jesus passed along the border of Samaria and Galilee. / As he entered a village / ten lepers went to meet him. / Keeping their distance / they raised their voices and said: / Jesus, Master, / have pity on us. / When he saw them he said: / Go / and show yourselves to the priests. / And on their way they were made clean. / One of them / realizing that he had been made clean, / returned praising God in a loud voice. / He threw himself face down at the feet of Jesus, / thanking him. / And this man was a Samaritan. / Jesus' comment was: / Were not ten made clean? / Where are the other nine? / Was no one found to return and give glory to God / except this stranger? / And he said to the man: / Stand up / and go your way; / your faith has saved you.

Read that passage first without any recognition of the phrase marks, then reread it with the use of vocal commas. Note the difference, the greater clarity, the distinctness. That is pace, and it is accomplished by practice.

Inability to hear the preacher and follow his remarks is a frequent complaint of people in the pews. Preachers, even those with years of experience, would be amazed to learn how much of their sermon remains unheard because it is poorly paced.

It is again a matter of control. The speaker must maintain control over his words so that they do not issue forth in a jumble; he must pace his words at the proper tempo. And this is accomplished chiefly by use of the vocal comma.

4. GESTURES.

Let us begin our discussion of gestures with an emphatic statement: Gestures are indispensable aids to communication for the public speaker.

However the gestures of which we are speaking are not the dramatic, arms-extended gestures of another age of oratory. The gestures of the Conversational Mode are those simple, human gestures that are made in front of the body, between the belt and the shoulders, with slight movements of the hands. These are the kind of gestures we all employ in our ordinary conversations, and they are the kind we must employ in public speaking to give it naturalness and vitality.

Make another experiment with a TV set. Turn off the sound during a commercial and observe the announcer attempting to sell his product. Without the intrusion of his words, you will be able to observe his gestures: the slight movement of his hands, the occasional pointed finger, the extended forearm as he reaches out to make a point. The announcer must make these gestures: he is attempting to present himself as a warm friend to the audience, someone who can inspire belief in his toothpaste, and the casual gesture is necessary to make him appear relaxed, sincere, communicative. Were he to stand before the television camera with his hands clenched at his sides, the image would be destroyed; and he would appear tense, rigid, and artificial.

Gesticulation, then, is necessary for effective human communication. It is necessary, first, for the speaker himself so that he can speak in the most natural and relaxed way possible, so that the whole man can enter into the process of communication. It is further necessary so that the preacher can channel and use the natural nervous energy that rises within him during a sermon. When the speaker gestures, he employs his nervous energy, works it off in the business of communication, makes it his servant; but when the speaker stands before an audience taut and rigid he bottles his nervousness up within himself, becomes its servant, and further increases his uneasiness.

Gesticulation is necessary, secondly, for the benefit of the audience. The people are more relaxed listening to a man who gestures, and they are more ready to believe what he says. He is communicating the impression of a confident, assured man who has something important to tell them and not a rigid wooden Indian who is reciting some memorized essay. It is interesting to observe that the audience does not consciously advert to the use of gesticulation, no more than we advert to the television announcer's use of gestures until we turn off the sound and study his gesticulation. And this is the way it should be, for gesticulation is a natural, expected element in human communication. But when gestures are absent the people in the audience do notice that they are being addressed by a tense, uncomfortable preacher, and this mood is unfortunately projected into the audience.

Rules for gesticulation? There are no true rules for gestures, since the gesture must be a natural movement employed to convey some thought or reenforce vocal expression. Gestures cannot be studied or planned, they must flow from the speaker's enthusiasm and desire to communicate. We can, though, offer some guide lines for gesticulation:

1. The most important element in gesticulation is the creation in the speaker's mind of the impulse to gesticulate. This is developed from his use of the Conversational Mode and his desire to communicate. As the speaker develops naturalness in the pulpit he should concomitantly bring into play the natural use of gestures. And as he develops his desire to communicate he should extend this into a desire to employ everything he has in getting his ideas across to the people—ideas, words, *and* gestures.

The speaker's fundamental thought about gestures should be: *I must gesture.*

2. As a negative bit of advice, do not attempt to prepare your gestures before you ascend the pulpit. Antique courses in elocution presented elaborate instructions about the gesture—it was "composed of three parts, preparation, stroke, relaxation." But this is futile and dangerous. Gestures should be spontaneous and natural.

A speaker who tries to plan his gesticulation will only make his gestures appear artificial and contrived. It is similar to the old story about the sexton who was cleaning the pulpit after Sunday services and discovered the manuscript of the pastor's sermon still on the lectern. He noticed some hand-written notes in the margin, and looking closer he found they said: "Argument weak here, pound like hell."

That never works.

3. To establish an initial basis for gesticulation, imagine a hollow box eighteen inches high sitting on top of the pulpit's lectern, and then exercise the impulse to gesture in that determined area. Make the natural small hand gestures you would customarily use in ordinary conversation while you are explaining something or driving home a point or asking a question.

It is probably better for the novice speaker to make no gestures at all for the first minute of his talk, but when he has settled himself he should begin to operate within the limits of that eighteen-inch box.

Any gesture is good as long as it is expressive and not distracting to the audience. Idiosyncrasies are part of a man, and therefore idiosyncratic gestures are not necessarily to be discouraged. President Kennedy punctuated his remarks with a jabbing finger during his press conferences, and the result was both expressive and individualistic. The only type gesture to be avoided is the one that annoys and distracts the audience, as would be, for example, the "Pontius Pilate routine"—that is, washing your hands in public by holding them clenched at your waist and then rubbing them together.

4. To study his gesticulation technique, the preacher might deliver part of a sermon before a mirror without actually articulating the words. During this pantomime he will be able to observe whether he is using gestures or not, and whether his gestures seem to say anything. If he finds he is using no gestures, he should make a determined effort during the pantomime to reinforce his remarks with gesticulation.

The preacher appears in the pulpit as a man speaking to other people, but he should appear as a whole man, and that implies animation, life, vitality. A large part of this is achieved through gesticulation. If he employs gestures he will have more confidence in himself, get more attention from his audience, and bestow more meaning on what he says.

5. PROJECTION.

We began our discussion of the Art of Public Speaking with the element of poise. It terminates here with a discussion of projection. And this is the proper order, because poise must terminate in projection to produce truly effective public speaking.

Projection is a combination of mental and vocal qualities which results in the speaker's voice being sharply and immediately directed at his audience. Retaining all of the control of the ASRM principle and all the naturalness of the Conversational Mode, the speaker should then project and direct and aim his voice at the audience. His voice must come out at the people and make them sit up and pay attention.

When you listen to a public speaker you can ascertain in the first three or four sentences whether the man is projective or not. The man who is nonprojective may use his voice correctly and modulate properly, but he is merely letting his voice fall over the edge of the pulpit unlike the projective speaker who pushes his voice directly at the people, taking care that it hits the ears of everyone in the room. Projection is evident in the speaker's voice, in his manner, in his whole person.

To insure projectivity, the public speaker should imagine that his voice is coming out of his mouth like tracer bullets which are being fired at a spot four feet from the floor on the back wall of the room in which he is speaking. Or, to use another example, he should hit the back wall like a baseball player slicing a line drive. He should not float his voice in an arc over the audience as if he were hitting a lazy fly ball.

This, therefore, is the basic rule for projection: select an imaginary spot four feet up the back wall, and *hit that back wall!*

The one danger to be avoided in hitting the back wall is the speaker's tendency to elevate his voice as he attempts to fill a larger room (the fly ball, instead of the line drive in our analogy). This not only dissipates the voice, making it thin and weak, but it also impairs the proper use of the ASRM principle. Accordingly, the speaker must project his voice on a straight line.

The novice speaker sometimes possesses a shyness or hesitancy in using projective techniques. It seems too demonstrative, too embarrassing. He would rather merely recite his sermon without being vocally direct and immediate. This diffidence or shyness or hesitancy, or whatever it may be, is fatal to successful public speaking. The preacher has to become dynamized with the desire to speak, he must have an urgency to communicate. To accomplish this he must put his message above his ego, he must subordinate any shyness to the importance of the work he is doing. St. Paul said that he became a fool for Christ, and the shy preacher may have to adopt that kind of thinking in order to employ projective techniques.

A word about the use of a microphone. The microphone is not a substitute for projection, but only an aid in its use. Most of our larger churches today employ some kind of public address system, and that is a fine thing, but the preacher must know how to use the system. There are a variety of types of microphones employed in the various public address systems with varying degrees of sensitivity. At the outset, the preacher should ascertain the sensitivity of the individual microphone he is using and then judge how far he must stand away from it to obtain the proper sound without a buzzing overtone. With some microphones the preacher must stand as close as eight or ten inches, but with a good one the usual distance is two feet.

Then the preacher should be certain that he is using enough volume with the microphone to be heard in every part of the church. He does not enjoy the situation of a radio or television broadcaster who has an engineer in a control booth to regulate the volume; he must do this by his own voice in conjunction with the public address system. He could study the faces of the people in the last row of the church—do they appear strained, as if they were having difficulty in hearing the speaker, or are they relaxed, comfortably listening to him?

But the capital point about the use of a microphone: you must still project and aim your voice at the back wall, using the microphone as an adjunct to your voice to give it the volume necessary to hit the wall.

All that we have said thus far about public speaking, from the structure of the speaker's mentality to the Conversational Mode, will remain largely ineffective if the preacher does not project his voice at the audience. Projection is the hallmark of the truly accomplished speaker: It distinguishes the man who gives a nice little talk from the dynamic speaker who captures the audience's attention and makes them listen.

Projection requires precious little practice. Merely the consistent use of our rule: Select an imaginary spot four feet up the back wall, and hit that back wall. The speaker can do this the first moment he opens his mouth in the pulpit, with no prolonged training, no sets of exercises. All he must do is remember to project at the audience.

And if he does, if he projects to the people, the audience is his.

To summarize the Conversational Mode: it is a natural, human way of speaking, based on the dynamics of conversational speech, and then extended to a larger audience with the necessary adjustments for group contact. It is comprised of five elements: modulation (the natural rhythm of human speech), variety (the occasional vocal changes used to augment expression and meaning), pace (the tempo necessary for speaking to a large group), and projection (direct vocal delivery to the large group).

EXERCISES

Remember the basic principle: Good contemporary public speaking is conversation projected.

The Conversational Mode:
1. *Modulation.*
    a. Make a searching appraisal of whether you are speaking with modulation, or whether perhaps you are using a monotone or singsong cadences. (Do not forget to be a "professional listener" to other people's sermons.)
    b. Rethink the principles of poise.
    c. Make a conscious effort to modulate. Practice by reading with expression, forcing modulation if necessary.
    Use our test sentences:
    > He is peculiar, but I *like* peculiar people. (up)
    > He who is not with me is *against* me. (down)
    • Say the word *Harry* with different inflections to change the meaning (question, imperative, disgust, amusement, attention, admiration, contempt, love.)
    • Do the same thing with the word *yes* (emphatic, evasive, enthusiastic, sarcastic, bored, annoyed, apprehensive, ecstatic.)
    • Recite the sentence "John gave the hat to Mary," and answer these questions by the inflection in your voice:

    > Who gave the hat to Mary?
    > To whom did John give the hat?
    > What did John give to Mary?
    > What did John do?

2. *Vocal Variety.*
    a. *Rate of Speed.*
    Read aloud, changing your rate of speed. Slow down to express more important ideas.
    b. *Volume.*
    Change the volume as you read aloud, increasing and decreasing the volume to create greater emphasis.

c. *Force.*

To gain the greatest amount of force, slow down and speak at a lower level of volume. Combine *a* and *b* as you read, and say it loudly and slowly.

d. *Pause.*

Create a "magic moment" by a three to five second pause —at the beginning of your talk, before an important idea, after an important idea.

3. *Pace.*

· Time your rate of speed by reading aloud for a short period, and then compute the word count. Are you in the general range of 120 to 160 words a minute?

· Use vocal commas, split-second pauses, to phrase your sentences and achieve proper tempo.

· Reread the annotated Gospel of Luke in this chapter, inserting a vocal comma at the phrase marks.

4. *Gestures.*

· Recognize the necessity of gesticulation for human communication: it makes the speaker feel natural, it channels his nervousness, it relaxes the audience.

· Say to yourself: I must gesture!

· Do not attempt to plan your gestures.

· Imagine a hollow box eighteen inches high sitting on top of the lectern, and exercise the impulse to gesture in that area.

· Employ the simple, human gestures of everyday speech: the outstretched hand, the pointed finger, the spread palms.

· Pantomime your talk before a mirror to see if you are reinforcing your remarks with gestures.

5. *Projection.*

· Remember that the final accomplishment of the Art of Public Speaking is to direct your voice immediately to the people.

· Study other speakers, and note the tremendous effectiveness of projective techniques.

· In public speaking, take an imaginary spot four feet from the floor on the back wall, and hit the back wall!

· Use the microphone as an aid to projection, and not a substitute for projection.

Review the principles of the Speaker's Mentality. (Recall how poise is lost, how it is regained. Review: desire, command, communication.)

Review the ASRM principle. (Recall how to coordinate the proper use of abdomen, shoulders, resonators, mouth.)

The combination of speaker's mentality, ASRM principle, and Conversational Mode makes the accomplished public speaker.

II

THE ART OF PERSUASION

1

THE SPEAKER'S GOAL: PERSUASION

This section of the book, the Art of Persuasion, is concerned with the planning, organization, and writing of the speaker's material so that he can accomplish his purpose of persuading the audience.

And that is our initial point: The speaker's fundamental goal in preparing his material should be to persuade his audience. He wants to communicate ideas, get the people to believe and accept what he is saying. We are not speaking of theological belief, but the belief of intellectual assent by which the people become convinced of the importance and truth of what he is saying. The speaker wants the audience to agree with his ideas, to say "Yes, yes" to his argument.

This seems obvious enough, but nonetheless many speakers are not sufficiently dynamized by this goal, they are not animated by an urgency to persuade the audience. They merely want to "give" their talk, recite their ideas to this audience. They do not grapple with the minds of the people for their assent nor press the argument until the people become convinced of it.

At the conclusion of a talk, a speaker should not content himself with the thought that the people listened to him. He should ask himself the further question: "But did they agree with me, accept what I was saying?" The effective public speaker is not satisfied with merely a hearing, he wants assent, he wants to persuade.

The entire talk or sermon must be constructed on the firm platform of the speaker's intent to persuade. If it is not, the talk will be weakened at every point, and the net result will be unsatisfactory: It will be missing that irreplaceable inner dynamism of persuasiveness.

Hence, before a speaker begins to compose his talk he needs to be sure that he is properly motivated, and this motivation must influence the entire area from his general purpose in preaching right down to his specific thesis for the particular sermon he is about to give.

Let us outline that motivation program:

1. GENERAL MOTIVATION.

The priest's enduring motivation for his preaching should emanate from his fundamental dedication as a priest. He has, as we indicated in Chapter 1 of the previous section, been commissioned by the Lord to preach. He must explain God's truth to the Christian people, convince them to accept Jesus as their Lord and friend, persuade them to do what the Lord wants. This should be his goading desire, his consuming passion, his urgent business. "I am in travail until Christ be formed in you," St. Paul said.

Alan Monroe, the celebrated professor of public speaking at Purdue University, has said that every public speaker must have the missionary spirit. Mr. Monroe was not speaking in an ecclesiastical sense, but in the sense that the public speaker must possess the missionary impulse to convert, to convince, to persuade, to gain assent for what he is saying. This, of course, is particularly applicable to the priest who is by vocation a missionary, someone sent to the people of God, someone who's business it is to persuade them of God's message.

What we are urging here is something the old rhetoricians used to call *pectus*, heart, that burning desire to convince. There is no substitute for *pectus*: If a man does not have it his sermon will be crippled. But if he possesses it, he will really communicate with the people, and they will be able to bestow on him that high encomium they sometimes say of preachers: "He is so sincere." And what they mean by that, of course, is that he seems to believe what he is saying and wants to get it across to us.

Preaching, therefore, cannot be an isolated experience in a priest's life, one of the functions he sometimes performs. It must flow from the very marrow of his life and dedication and belief. Karl Rhaner has written: "Testifying to the faith is, in general, essentially connected with the preacher's genuine witness in his own life, in other words, with his holiness."

This genuine witness in his own life is concretized in the specific act of preaching in which the priest is engaged. It is here that he has the opportunity to persuade the people of God. And he must think of it in terms of opportunity. He must be completely existential about it, realizing that this sermon before this congregation on this particular day can never be preached again in the history of the world. Here is his opportunity to persuade, and he must not lose it.

This is the kind of general motivation the priest should bring to his sermon.

2. SPECIFIC MOTIVATION.

a. *Topic*. The topic is the precise subject of the day's sermon, the particular section of Christian truth the priest is going to discuss.

In Part III we will delineate some aspects of the essential Christian message the priest should preach, therefore let us stipulate now that he chooses some topic. The Eucharist, for example.

The problem is that at this point some preachers begin the composition of their sermon. But that is unfortunate because the subject matter is not determined precisely enough. It must be further clarified. It must be stated in a thesis.

b. *Thesis*. Every sermon or talk should be constructed on a proposition, an argument, something the speaker is trying to explain, or convince the people of, or encourage them to do. This is called the thesis, the precise statement of the argument.

The speaker's business is to persuade, and accordingly he is attempting to induce the people in his audience to make a practical judgment about the material in his sermon. Hence he must be able to put that practical judgment in words in the form of a thesis before he begins the composition of the sermon. Then he will know where he is going as he organizes and delivers his material. The thesis itself does not necessarily have to be stated during the sermon, but it serves as the basis for the development of the speaker's argument.

We selected the Eucharist as an illustrative topic. Let us now state that in a precise thesis, because as it stands it is too vague and too broad for a preacher to work with. One aspect of the Eucharist we might discuss in a particular sermon is frequent reception of the sacrament. Our thesis, then, might be: Frequent reception of the Eucharist.

But that is still too vague. It suffers from one of the fundamental defects of contemporary preaching: it is not sufficiently audience-related, it is not directed immediately to a present audience, it is too Olympian. We will discuss this aspect of relevancy in the following chapter, but for the moment let us state that the speaker's material must be audience-related and audience-directed. Otherwise there is the frequent danger that the preacher will be merely giving a verbal essay, rather than speaking to the people in his audience, trying to persuade them of something.

Relating our thesis to the audience, we may now state it this way: It is important that we receive the Lord frequently in the Eucharist. The thesis thus stated summarizes the principal argument of our sermon about the Eucharist. It is the theme of the sermon and the truth about which we are trying to persuade the audience. We should be similarly able to summarize into a single-sentence thesis the argument of the usual Sunday sermon of seven to ten minutes. Longer discourses may require a fuller diagram to embrace the argument, but the average short talk demands a precise one-sentence statement. It is the way to gain coherency, clarity, intelligibility.

Many preachers are unable to summarize their sermons in one sentence, and this is an undeniable indication that they have not mastered their material. It is too vague, too disorganized, too fuzzy in their own minds. They have not synthesized their material, selected the key idea, or decided what they are really trying to tell their audience. They choose a general topic, and then just talk about it, a little of this and a little of that. They are not trying to persuade the audience of some precise truth. The preacher should be aware of this fact: *If you, the preacher, are unable to summarize your sermon in one thesis, then the audience is certainly unable to do it.* If it is too vague and disorganized for you to give it a precise statement, then it is too vague and disorganized for the audience to follow. The argument must flow from the mind of the speaker into the minds of his listeners, but if it proceeds from the speaker's mind in a disorganized manner it will be received in a disorganized manner, if it is received at all.

The thesis is the organized statement of the principal idea of the sermon. It is therefore the point at which the composition of the sermon should begin. Sermons and talks should be constructed organically, that is, starting with the thesis and building the sermon around that. You should not compose a sermon like the little boy who is writing a composition for school: he takes a piece of paper, then laboriously writes the first sentence. Ah, he has one sentence finished, he thinks. Then he writes another sentence. Two sentences done now. Then a third sentence, and a fourth, until twenty-five or thirty sentences are on the paper and the composition is completed. What you most often have is merely a compilation of sentences rather than a precise, driving argument. This is *not* the way to compose a sermon, although unfortunately many sermons are composed that way. Organic composition demands that the speaker form a precise thesis and then build upon that, developing it, explaining it, illustrating it, providing inspiration and motivation. We will discuss this process more fully in the following chapter, but for our purposes in this chapter let us remember that the sermon develops organically from the extension of the thesis.

c. *Personalized Thesis.* There is one further refinement of the thesis that better establishes the speaker-listener relationship and that we might call the personalized thesis, a statement of the argument in terms of the speaker's motivation to persuade.

In our example the thesis is: It is important that we receive the Lord frequently in the Eucharist. This can now be taken one step further and stated: I am going to persuade these people that it is important for them to receive the Lord frequently in the Eucharist.

The thesis is then related both to the speaker's goal and to the actual audience. It embraces three elements: the speaker, the precise thesis, and the audience. It is the ultimate in motivation.

Any thesis can be similarly stated by personalizing it, stating it in terms of the speaker's intent to persuade people of his thesis. "I am going to persuade these people that . . ." This is the kind of thesis that has life and fire, that really leaps out at the people and makes them give assent to the speaker's argument.

In summary, the speaker's fundamental goal is persuasion, and he accomplishes this by motivating himself. The general motivation provides his enduring mentality, while the specific motivation establishes the speaker's topic, his thesis, and his personalized thesis.

EXERCISES

Remember: The speaker's goal is persuasion.
Ask yourself: Do people merely listen to my talk, or do they agree with me, accept what I am saying?

1. *General Motivation.*
   • The priest's function is to preach, to persuade people of God's word.

- You must have Alan Monroe's "spirit of missionary."
- Be sincere, have *pectus*, try to convince.
- One sermon is of incalculable value, an opportunity that will never occur again in the history of the world.

2. *Specific Motivation.*

   a. *Thesis.*

   - State your topic in a precise thesis, an argument that you are presenting to the people.
   - Make your thesis audience-related.
   - Be able to summarize the principal argument of the sermon in your thesis. (Remember: If you are unable to summarize your sermon in one thesis, it is too vague for the audience to follow.)
   - Use the thesis as the basis for building your sermon organically.

   b. *Personalized Thesis.*

   - Personalize your thesis by stating it in terms of the speaker-listener relationship—"I am going to persuade these people that . . ."

Continue to review and practice the principles of Part I, The Art of Public Speaking.

2

HOW TO ORGANIZE YOUR SERMON: THE FERM PRINCIPLE

The thesis constitutes the speaker's basic argument, but he must then develop it into a cogent and persuasive talk. It is here that he may get into difficulties and lose control of his material. He might merely put together a conglomeration of ideas, with a dash of this and a dash of that, perhaps throw in an anecdote or two, and then recite this to the audience. The result is a rambling sermon without plan or order. The people find it hard to follow this type sermon. They become quickly bored. They remain unconvinced.

The speaker needs to organize his talk. He must marshal his ideas, arrange them, sift them, present them in an intelligent and convincing and appealing order.

Here is a ready plan for organizing your talk:

Tell them the facts. (Facts)
Explain them. (Explanation)
Show how it is important to the audience. (Relevancy)
Tell them what to do about it. (Motivation)

Facts, Explanation, Relevancy, Motivation—these constitute something we might call the FERM principle, an ordered sequence for the development of a thesis.

The FERM principle contains the four elements that should be included in every persuasive talk. The speaker has to present his facts, then he must explain them, show what they mean, clarify them. And he must relate all this to the people, tell them why it is important and necessary to believe this thing or do that thing or avoid the other thing. Finally he must convince them to do something about it. If he communicates these four points, he has presented a clear and coherent argument; he will necessarily have persuaded his audience.

The FERM principle is also a ready outline for simply and quickly constructing a talk or sermon. It is an all-purpose outline that can be used for almost any talk. The speaker can assemble his material and then develop it along the guide lines of the outline— Facts, Explanation, Relevancy, and Motivation. And, behold, you have an intelligent and persuasive sermon!

It should be noted, however, that the FERM principle does not include the introduction or conclusion. It contains only what in an older rhetoric we formerly called The Body of the talk. The introduction and conclusion can, and very often should be composed after the thesis has been developed through this principle. First develop your argument, then you can construct an engaging introduction and a sharp conclusion.

Nor is it necessary to present the elements of the FERM principle in the precise order that they are stated. The order of parts may be inverted and rearranged. Sometimes, for example, you might start with the Motivation, and then cite the Facts and Explanation and Relevancy. Or another time you might begin with the Relevancy. Any order is satisfactory provided that the order is interesting and intelligible. The important consideration is that all four elements be included.

The various elements may differ in length, too. In some sermons it might be necessary to expend the greatest amount of time on the Explanation. In others the Motivation might demand the most time. Or in others the Relevancy. In some sermons you might be able to handle one or other of the elements in a few sentences. The elements of the FERM principle are not necessarily to be divided into four equal parts.

The principle can be accommodated to almost any talk because it satisfies all the needs in the minds of the audience. It tells us what to think, and what to do about it. In the old homiletics, sermons were classified as either Dogmatic or Moral: the Dogmatic sermon treating of something to be believed, and the Moral of something to do. This is an arbitrary and unreal division. Every sermon should include both elements, informing us how to think about something and how to relate this to our daily lives. If we preach a Dogmatic sermon, confining ourselves entirely to the way this truth should be grasped by the mind and not describing its impact on the person's life, we are giving a lecture, not a sermon. And if we preach a Moral sermon, and merely tell the people what they cannot do, without describing the reasons for it in God's revelation and then integrating it into the whole Christian life, we are only proclaiming moralisms.

But let us examine the four steps of the FERM principle:

1. FACTS.

In this step the speaker should present the truths he is discussing. If he is giving a homily, he will tell the Scripture story, or at least the parts of it that are pertinent. If his topic is some aspect of the Christian life, he will describe it and show its place in Christian life. If he is discussing a problem, he will state it, indicating the difficulties. In brief, he is getting the issues on the board.

We might note that the preacher needs to present vital and intelligent facts: He must know Scripture in order to state it; he must have an understanding of the Christian life; and he must be able to see real problems when they occur. This demands that a priest be conversant with the facts of religion, by reading the Scriptures and by reading the Christian authors, old and new. If a priest confines his reading to a few illustrated magazines and the sports pages of a newspaper, he is severely limiting his potential as a speaker. The priest is, whether he is ready to admit it or not, committed to a communication art: He is obliged to stand before a large group of people each week and deliver a talk, commenting on the issues of Christianity as they are applied to the contemporary scene. To do this he must be a man of reflection. He must read, think, discuss. If he does not, he will almost inevitably talk about platitudinous things or trivialities or inanities. The priest needs facts to present to the Christian people. He must spend the time to search them out.

2. EXPLANATION.

The facts of the sermon require explanation. They must be clarified, elucidated, made intelligible to the audience. In a homily the preacher needs to explain the Scripture, show what it means. Discussing the parable of the sower and the seed, for example, the preacher must explain the extended metaphor Christ is using and show the meaning of the sower, the seed, the various types of soil described in the parable. In discussing the Christian life he must explain and define what he is talking about. A discussion of Christian hope, for example, should define hope, show what it is, what it is not, describe its implications.

While the preacher should not talk down to the people in his audience, neither should he take too much for granted. It is always advisable to define and explain what you are talking about, even if this is accomplished in only a few sentences. Be clear, and your audience will be able to follow you.

The preacher has a particular obligation to explain and be clear because his education and background have made him a professional in the field of religion. He has studied his religion from the viewpoint of scholastic philosophy and scientific theology, and he is, perhaps unwittingly, in the position of a professional talking to non-professionals about his field. He therefore must take special effort to explain his material and make it understandable to the audience. He is in somewhat the position of an atomic scientist who has been asked to give a talk about atomic fusion to a Rotary Club luncheon. The scientist is a professional talking to nonprofessionals, and he must present his material accordingly. He cannot give his talk in the same manner and with the same vocabulary he would use addressing a university lecture. He has to use concepts and analogies and vocabulary that are familiar to his audience. He might perhaps explain the atomic field as a group of oranges floating in a circumscribed area—not exactly accurate, but it is analagous to the reality and comprehensible to the particular audience. Were he to talk in scientific jargon about neutrons and protons, his audience would be unable to follow him. The priest must similarly remember that he is a professional and he has to explain his material carefully to his lay audience, not speaking down to them but relating his material to them in concepts and vocabulary that are familiar to them.

The average priest is usually unaware of how much technical jargon he uses in his sermon and how little this is understood by the audience. You frequently hear something like this from a pulpit: "Let us outline the dispositions necessary for the fruitful reception of the Eucharist." That is clear enough—for the priest, not the layman. The preacher has to translate that phrase into something comprehensible and contemporary, like: "Here are the things you have to do to get the most out of the Eucharist." Or: "If you really want to make communion count, here is what you have to do." Or anything else, provided it be stated in intelligent and intelligible language, and not the cant of scientific theology.

If a physician were giving a lecture to a group of doctors he might state: "My most interesting patient last year was one who had a fractured patella." But were he addressing a group of laymen he would have to say: "My most interesting patient last year was one who had a broken knee." He would have to use popular terms and not his professional jargon.

The preacher is in the same situation. And the terms "necessary dispositions" and "fruitful reception" are as technical in his profession as the word "patella" is for the doctor.

Hence, a rule: *Beware of the preacher's "patella."*

Also, although the priest should speak authoritatively and convincingly in his explanation, he should not give the impression that he has the answers to all questions. Nor should he indicate that he can explain everything about life from the pages of Scripture. That would be untrue and ultimately harmful to his message.

God has revealed to us certain things about life—the most basic things, certainly: the meaning of life, our eternal destiny, our relationship with God, our relationship with other human beings. The Scriptures are a handbook of God's revelation, a compendium of things we must know and do to live according to his plan. It does not provide the answer for every one of life's questions, although some preachers talk about it as if it did. Do you think the Scriptures can tell us everything? Where, then, do you find an explanation for these questions: Why is a small child inflicted with cerebral palsy? Why is the wife who longs to have children found to be sterile? Why does God give the gift of faith to this man and not to the other? You might point out texts that tell us we must trust in the goodness of God. But that is not an explanation, only an act of confidence in God that there is an explanation in his plan that he will unfold to us someday after the present life.

It is good for the preacher to present himself to the people as a humble coseeker of truth. He knows the word of God and he explains it to the people, but there are certain questions that must be committed to the goodness of God. The people have confidence in a man who speaks like that: He is speaking the truth. But the preacher who has a facile answer for everything is inevitably speaking in platitudes: He has a cliché for every question that arises. His performance has a hollow ring about it, and the people do not believe him.

To summarize: Explain the facts of the sermon, help the people understand what you are talking about, clarify your material. But do it in a nontechnical way, approaching your material as a humble and intelligent human being.

3. RELEVANCY.

Lack of relevancy is usually the major fault in the contemporary preacher's material. What he says is true and correct, but it is not audience-related, it is not directed to the people. Such a preacher gives the impression that he knows a lot of theology but precious little about people.

A vintage story recounts the dialogue between two old Irish housewives as they leave church one Sunday:

> BRIDGET: Ah, Mary, that priest is a fine young boy, isn't he?
>
> MARY: He is. And wasn't it a lovely sermon he preached about marriage?
>
> BRIDGET: Indeed it was. And I wish I knew as little about it as he does.
>
> MARY: True, bless him.

Bridget's reaction is unfortunately shared by many people: that the preacher's sermon is edifying, but has little relation to their practical lives. The people feel that the preacher is not addressing himself to their situation, that he is living and thinking in an ivory tower, divorced from the real world, Olympian.

The preacher must obtain his material from the revelation of God, but he must *apply* it to the people who listen to him. He needs to make his doctrine audience-related. He has to think it out in terms of their comprehension and needs. He has to make the people feel that he understands their situation. Only then will his message have impact on their lives.

Jesus Christ should be the inspiration and model for every preacher: He is the preacher *par excellence* of all time. If we preached as He did, we would be perfect preachers. Examine the method of His preaching—it is preeminently audience-related. Christ did not speak in the stylized forms of His time: not the legalistic, moralistic speaking of the Roman world to the west, nor the obtuse, philosophical speaking of the Greek world to the east. He spoke in a human fashion to the audience that was listening to Him. He spoke about lost sheep and lilies of the field and fig trees and unmerciful servants and a prodigal son. He used the common facts of life to demonstrate his truth: coins and salt and sparrows, wedding feasts and banquets and vineyards. And the people understood him. He was speaking to *them*. He understood their lives. Christ preached objective truth, but He preached it in terms of things His audience could understand. What more could you demand in a preacher?

To make his sermon more audience-related, the preacher should take his facts—the Scripture, the theology, the liturgy—and make them relevant to his contemporary audience. It is not sufficient to merely announce the word of God, it must be applied and directed to this audience listening to him. The preacher must call on his store of knowledge about people and their lives, and think out his material against this background. The priest who spends his week dealing with people, listening to their problems, seeing their difficulties, helping them in their crises, and then steps into the pulpit on Sunday morning and utters a few banal platitudes is not using his total experience. He is not addressing these people with the same mentality he used during the week: he has made religion a sacristy experience rather than a relevant, burning, vital force in their lives.

There are two techniques the preacher might employ in the preparation of his sermon to enhance relevancy. First, he might construct in his mind an imaginary member of the audience to whom he can direct the sermon. And let him construct a complete image. For example, he might form the picture of a man, thirty-seven years old, married for fourteen years, father of five children ranging from three to twelve. He is an insurance agent, travels to his job each day by commuter train. He lives in a twenty-two thousand dollar house, has a second mortgage on it. He is deeply devoted to his family, although he is beginning to experience difficulty communicating with his twelve-year-old boy. His marriage has had a few rough spots, but he and his wife have adjusted satisfactorily to each other, despite the fact that there are moments when he feels he cannot understand her at all. He worries about that second mortgage and his mother-in-law whom he has been supporting in a nursing home for the past four years. If you asked him, he would say that he is happy enough, but he wonders what the future will bring.

Now—it is to *this* man the preacher must speak, this man who is worried about the second mortgage, who is having problems communicating with his son. What does the preacher have to tell him? What does he need to know about God's revelation? What can he say to him that is pertinent and relevant?

Let the preacher keep the image of his thirty-seven-year-old man in front of him as he thinks about his sermon and begins to organize the material. Speak to him! Tell him things! Communicate with him! Don't merely prepare a sermon on the Eucharist, for example, but instead tell *him* about the Eucharist in a way he can understand and appreciate.

A second technique for relevancy consists in directing your material to typical questions that may lurk in the minds of your audience. As the preacher examines his material, he could profitably ask himself the questions that the average listener might ask about that material. For example, if the preacher were preparing a sermon on the love of God, he might attempt to project himself into the mind of his listeners. What questions or objections or difficulties could they have about the love of God? Well, perhaps the first question might be: How can you love someone you cannot see? Or a sermon on bearing with one's crosses and difficulties might raise this question: If God loves us, why does he allow us to suffer?

Then in composing his sermon, the preacher could develop his remarks with those questions in mind. He does not have to state the questions as such, nor should he make his sermon a rebuttal of difficulties. His remarks should be stated in a positive way, but against the background of the real difficulties. In the sermon on the love of God, the preacher could describe how we can love God, even though we cannot see him visibly. And in the sermon on bearing with one's problems, he could develop the point about the value of suffering and why God does allow us to suffer. In this way there is a meeting of minds: The preacher is actually addressing himself to the real condition of his listeners. There is relevancy.

In addition to these two principal techniques of relevancy, there are four short verbal devices for injecting relevancy into your sermon:

a. *The use of the word you.* If the speaker employs the word *you* in his sermon he is increasing his relevancy. It implies that he is talking to the audience, directing his remarks to them.

b. *Questions.* The statement of a question directed to the audience is also valuable. For example, something like this: "My friends, let me ask you a question—what is the most important thing in your life?"

c. *Challenge.* A direct challenge to the audience creates immediacy. An example: "My friends, try an experiment—tomorrow try to say something kind to every person you meet."

d. *Cogitation.* An important thought phrased in the form of a rhetorical question brings the speaker and his audience together. An example: "Did you ever think that seventy-five years from today, every person in this church this morning will be dead?"

To make his sermon audience-related, the preacher has to think out his material in terms of his audience. He has to project himself into the minds of his listeners. He has to think of their situation, their needs, their problems. In a word, he has to have empathy. The classic example of empathy is the news photograph of the pole-vaulting event at a track meet: the pole vaulter is at the moment of pushing himself up over the cross bar fifteen feet above the ground; and in the background a group of spectators are watching him intently, and a number of them have one leg lifted off the ground helping the athlete. This is empathy, a mental projection into the situation and consciousness of another. This is the spirit the preacher should bring to the preparation of his material, a feeling and a sensitivity for the people in his audience. Only in this way will the important things he has to say have impact in their lives.

Remember: the preacher must have empathy. *He must keep one leg lifted off the ground!*

In summary: Lack of relevancy is usually the major defect in sermons. We must, therefore, preach as Christ preached—objective truth directed to the audience's needs and comprehension. To increase his relevancy the priest should construct in his mind a typical member of his audience, and then direct the material to him; and he should pose to himself the questions his listeners might conceivably raise about the sermon's topic matter. Finally, he needs empathy; he must get into the minds of his listeners.

4. MOTIVATION.

The final step in the process of persuasion consists in convincing the people in your audience to take some action on the matter you have been discussing. This action may take a number of different forms: something to do, something to avoid, something to accept as part of one's future thinking.

The sermon or talk is unsuccessful if at the completion the listener merely says to himself, "Very nice." He must say, "Yes, I will do that, or avoid the other thing, or believe that." The speaker's whole performance is directed to obtaining that *yes* from his listener.

If the preacher has done his job well up to this point—if he has posited his facts, explained them clearly, and made them important and relevant—then his task of audience motivation is half done. He has brought his listeners to a logical point where they will want to do what he suggests. But he must suggest it to them, he must tell them what to do.

For complete effectiveness, audience motivation should be both positive and practical:

a. *Positive.* Many speakers fail to motivate their audience properly because they are not direct and emphatic in this part of their talk. They perhaps have explained their material clearly and made it important to the audience, but then they fail to nail down the argument. They seem to say, "Well, there it is—lots of luck!"

The people need to be told how to make this information dynamic and effective in their lives. They need to be told the practical implications of the material that has been explained to them. To accomplish this the preacher must speak forthrightly and emphatically, without equivocation or hesitancy.

b. *Practical.* Audience motivation, however, should be practical and not platitudinous. You should offer clear, precise, effective directives to the audience.

At this final stage of the sermon the preacher can allow his material to get away from him by becoming vague and indefinite and imprecise. If he has been speaking about the love of God, he might allow his remarks to drift off into something like this: "Well, let's love God, because it is important." But how do you love God? What are you supposed to do? Tell them. Outline it for them. Show them how they can love God in their daily lives. Or if he has been speaking about reception of the Eucharist, he should clearly and precisely tell them how to make it effective—how to prepare themselves for it, what to do during Mass, what to do when they actually receive the Body of Christ.

Precise audience motivation should not be restricted only to those sermons and talks in which you are encouraging some specific and determined course of action. Even those talks that are designed only for changing the audience's mentality demand precise motivation. If, for example, you are discussing the parable of the weeds in St. Matthew's Gospel, your intention undoubtedly is to explain the presence of evil in the world, employing Christ's illustration of the weeds sown among the crop. But at the motivation step in your sermon you must, in so many words, tell the people that this is how they are to think about evil, this is how they are to react when they are confronted by the overwhelming calamities of our times, this is how they are to maintain their equilibrium. You must nail it down, you must give the people something to take away with them.

This demands that the speaker think his material through to the ultimate point of relevancy. And it demands that his directives be realistic and effective, directed to the practical situation in which the people of your audience live. It is comparatively easy to push a platitude out at the audience, but it requires some attention and consideration to make your material realistically practical. A preacher might say: "God wants us to love everybody." That is true enough, but the preacher is leaving it up in the air dangerously close to the area of the platitudinous. He must be more precise and more practical. How do you love everybody? How *can* you love everybody? What must I do in my daily life—tomorrow!—to love all the people I encounter?

To increase audience motivation, the preacher might again invoke the image of the typical listener that he constructed during the relevancy step. Think of that thirty-seven-year-old man with the second mortgage. Tell him what he must do to make this material practical and efficacious in his life. Give him precise and realistic directives. Do not merely float platitudes at him. Relate the application of your material to his real, work-a-day life. Then you will be telling your audience something that is useful and realistic.

In summary: motivation is the action step in the process of persuasion; it tells your audience what to do about the material you have been discussing. But your motivation must be both positive and practical. If there is a motivation step in your sermon it keeps your material audience-related throughout the talk, and it prevents it from descending into the area of the platitude.

The FERM principle contains the essential elements needed in a persuasive talk: facts, explanation, relevancy, and motivation. Every talk should include these elements, although not necessarily in the sequence we have stated them here. But if a talk does not present the facts, explain them, make them relevant to the audience, and move the audience to some form of action, then that talk is not truly convincing and persuasive.

The FERM principle is furthermore a real, all-purpose outline that can be used by both the novice and the experienced speaker to compose, quickly and effectively, a talk that has impact and dynamism.

EXERCISES

Organize your talk along the lines of the FERM principle:
1. *Facts.*
    · Get the issues on the board, state the facts plainly and clearly.
2. *Explanation.*
    · Clarify your facts, explain them.
    · Do not take too much for granted: define what you are talking about.
    · Beware of the preacher's *patella*, the technical and professional jargon.
    · Examine your material as a humble seeker of truth: do not try to explain away what cannot be explained away, or else you will be indulging in clichés.
3. *Relevancy.*
    · Make your material audience-related.
    · Preach solid truth, but apply it to your audience.
    · Construct in your imagination a typical member of your audience, and speak to *him.*
    · Ask yourself the questions a typical member of your audience might ask about your topic, and then direct the positive statement of your material toward these real questions.
    · Use the short verbal devices for relevancy: the word *you;* questions; challenge; cogitation.

• Project yourself into the minds of your audience; have empathy—keep one leg lifted off the ground.

• Take Jesus, the preacher, as your model—he preached the most profound truth, but he applied it to his real audience.

4. *Motivation.*

• Tell your audience what to do about the facts you have been discussing.

• Make your audience motivation positive: tell them directly and emphatically what they must do.

• Make it practical: give precise and effective directives, not mere platitudes.

• Reconstruct the image of your typical listener, and tell him what he must do in his real world.

• Ask yourself: At the conclusion of my sermon do the people say, "Very nice," or do they say, "*Yes,* I will do that, or avoid that, or believe that."

Continue to review the principles and exercises of Part I, and co-ordinate these with the FERM principle.

3

INTRODUCTIONS AND CONCLUSIONS

The introduction and conclusion of a talk deserve separate attention because they can be composed after the main section of the sermon had been organized, and because they perform a special and distinct function.

In the composition of his talk, the speaker should first select his thesis and then develop it according to the ordered sequence of the FERM principle. It is perhaps more effective to compose the introduction and conclusion after the theme has been persuasively developed by the FERM principle. At that point, the speaker can begin to devise ways to introduce his material and conclude it, and thereby gain the particular effect and impact these parts can contribute to his talk.

A. INTRODUCTIONS.

The purpose of the introduction is to capture the audience's attention. The older rhetoric maintained that the purpose of the introduction was to provide a prestatement of the argument, an opening presentation of what the speaker was going to prove. But that is not quite accurate. The chief function of this part of the talk is to engage the people in the audience, to gain their attention so they will listen to the speaker. In fact, a prestatement of the thesis is so pedantic that it can immediately destroy audience interest. It is more effective to intrigue the people at the outset and keep them guessing for a few moments about the direction you are taking.

The opening moments of a talk are critical: If you engage the people immediately, you have taken a quick and important step toward persuasion. But if you lose them at the outset, if you start so

slowly that they do not give you their attention, it may take minutes to engage them again, if at all.

We mentioned in Part I that the preacher should pause a few
seconds at the very beginning of his talk in order to draw the attention of the entire audience. Then, when he has the attention of
everyone in the room focused on him, he should begin his talk,
crisply and sharply. The first fifteen seconds of the talk are the
crucial ones—this is the time when you either engage the people
and hold their interest, or allow them to slump back in their seats,
indifference written all over their faces.

Hence, a principle: *The first fifteen seconds of a talk are crucial;
do not let the audience slip away from you during that time!*

How do you engage their attention? There are a number of ways,
but the principle underlying them all may be best illustrated by a
technique used in articles appearing in popular magazines. An author of such an article has the same problem as the speaker: he
must get attention immediately, or else he will not have any audience. (In the case of the author, he will lose his audience by the
fact that people will simply turn the page, while in the speaker's
case his audience will "turn him off" inside their heads.) Notice the
technique employed in many magazines: Instead of beginning the
article in a slow, didactic style, the author makes a quick thrust for
audience interest. In an article about traffic fatalities in the United
States, for instance, the author might begin:

> George Dunne backed his new station wagon out of
> the garage next to his home in suburban Detroit. It
> was Christmas eve, 1964, and the rear of the car was
> filled with brightly wrapped presents. Sitting next to
> George Dunne was his fifteen-year-old son, Billy, a
> sophomore in high school. They were on their way to
> bring presents to Billy's grandmother. It was the last
> trip they would ever take. . . .

And after this introduction, which cites a case history, the article
might develop into a discussion of the forty-five thousand traffic
deaths each year. This is a faster and more interesting start than
something like:

> In this article, we are going to discuss traffic fatalities
> in America. Each year there are many of these. It is
> important that Americans realize that . . .

In the first illustration, there is evident a strong intent to interest, to attract, to get the reader to continue; while in the second, there is only a weary and uninteresting inception of an article.

This is the same underlying principle that should operate in the introduction of a talk. Although the introduction in the spoken word will not be perhaps quite as contrived as the one in the article, it should share the same intent: an attempt to capture attention.

This can be achieved in several ways, among them:

1. *Question.* Asking the audience a question in the opening sentence incites interest and engages the people. A start like this engages: "My friends, do you know what is the most horrible sin you could possibly commit?"

2. *Story.* An anecdote always attracts attention, whether it concerns some historical figure, some unknown figure, or the speaker himself.

3. *Quotation.* Some quotation that is incisive and thought-provoking can serve to intrigue the audience.

The introduction should not be too lengthy, since you want to move on to the development of your thesis. But it should be sharp, a quick thrust for attention. If you are dull and didactic in your introduction, you are lost. How often have you heard sermons begin like this:

> In the economy of our salvation, my dear friends, the Incarnation is a prime and fundamental truth which . . .

> Today we are going to speak about divine grace. Grace is a quality inherent in the soul and . . .

> In today's Gospel, my dear friends, we once again have the privilege of watching Christ work one of his miracles. Now, a miracle is something beyond the ordinary power of man. It . . .

Those introductions are ponderous and oppressive. They do not engage you, or make you want to listen with interest and enthusiasm. But why not something like this for quick interest:

> Two years ago I was standing outside St. Peter's Basilica in Rome when I noticed a Cardinal alighting from a nearby automobile. He was tall, dressed in the full regalia of a Cardinal—and he was a Negro.

William James, the renowned American psychologist, once said that the art of being wise is the art of knowing what to overlook.

Let me ask you a question: Do you know God? I don't mean know about Him from books and sermons, but know Him as a person, face to face, just the way you know your brother or sister.

This morning I'd like to tell you a story about the most courageous man I ever knew. Let's call him John Smith, because that wasn't his name.

The engaging introduction requires that the preacher study his material carefully. He must ask himself: What can I say here to capture attention? It takes a little extra time and effort to compose an engaging introduction, but it repays you that priceless dividend: a hearing from your audience.

Remember, those first fifteen seconds of your sermon are crucial. You must get the attention of your audience. And for that you need a sharp and interesting introduction.

B. CONCLUSION.

The basic function of the sermon's conclusion is to maintain and provide some continuance for the total impact of the talk. If the conclusion is poor, if the speaker allows the fire and dynamism of his talk to drain off into a weak and hesitant finish, the enduring effect of his message will be greatly diminished.

Presuming that the speaker has engaged and motivated his audience throughout his talk, he now needs a strong finish. How unfortunate it is when the speaker breaks the spell near the end of the talk and almost seems to negate the urgency of the things he has been talking about. A vital message demands a vital finish.

Many conclusions convey this impression: "Well, that's about it, so I guess I'd better stop here." This is a flat, ho-hum ending that leaves a bad taste lingering in the listeners' mouths. Rather than ending with a sharp, incisive conclusion, the speaker seems to have run out of enthusiasm. And the effect on the audience is disastrous: They catch the speaker's mood of uncertainty, and this flavors their later recollection of the sermon.

You want your audience to say *yes, yes* right till the very end of the sermon, and you want this spirit of affirmation to remain in their minds. The way to accomplish this is to finish strongly and sharply, because your conclusion is the final thing your listeners carry away with them.

Here are some principles that should guide the composition of your conclusion:

1. The conclusion must be carefully prepared, with the realization that it is your last opportunity for persuasion. Plan your ending deliberately, and do not merely sputter to a stop like an automobile running out of gas.

2. Employ your imagination, and avoid a trite ending. Ecclesiastical speakers often use the "lettuce course ending"—let us do this, let us do that, let us do the other thing. That is trite and unimaginative.

3. Make your ending brief. Many speakers wind around and around like an airplane looking for a place to land. This wearies the people in the audience, and makes them begin to yearn desperately for you to stop.

And some specific ways to conclude your sermon:

1. *Quotation*. A quotation that you may or may not have used in the body of the sermon often provides a good ending and a precise restatement of your thesis. In a sermon on Christian love, you might say:

> "And remember what the usually mild St. John says in his epistle—'If anyone says he loves God, and does not love his neighbor, that man is a liar.'"

2. *Summary*. A brief recapitulation of the two or three main points of your talk can conclude it effectively. This gives the audience a quick review of your argument and enables you to end in the full vigor of your persuasiveness.

3. *Question*. Ending with a question keeps your audience with you until the final second. For example:

> "Our Lord tells us that whatever we do to anyone else, we do to him. Tomorrow you will encounter Christ many times in your day—in the person of all the men and women and children you meet. Will you recognize Him?"

4. *Appeal to Action*. A direct appeal to action at the end of the talk carries the motivation step through the conclusion. It is a persuasive way to conclude a sermon. For example:

"Jesus told us that He is taking care of us, just as He takes care of the birds of the air and lilies of the field. He asks us not to worry. This is his pledge to us. Trust Him. Put your confidence in Him. He won't let you down."

There are many other ways to conclude a sermon—challenge, oratorical climax, restatement of the thesis—but they are all predicated on the same principle: the sermon's conclusion must be sharp and incisive.

Control, as we noted much earlier, is a key factor in public speaking. The speaker must maintain control throughout the entire talk, up to and including the conclusion. If he allows his control to dissolve at the conclusion, he can nullify much of the good he has accomplished during the talk. But if his conclusion has snap and impact, the people in the audience will take the sermon home with them. And that is what the preacher wants.

EXERCISES

A. *Introduction.*

· Remember: the first fifteen seconds of your sermon are crucial; do not allow the audience to slip away from you during that time!

· Remember: the purpose of an introduction is to capture the audience's attention.

· Ask yourself: What can I say to capture attention?

· Employ some of the introduction techniques:

1. *Question.* Pose a direct question to the audience in the opening sentence.

2. *Story.* Begin with a story to attract immediate human interest.

3. *Quotation.* An apt and thought-provoking quotation can intrigue the audience.

B. *Conclusion.*

· Remember: the purpose of the conclusion is to provide some form of continuing impact for your message.

· Do not bring your talk to a hesitant, fumbling, awkward finish; but rather:

· Prepare your conclusion carefully, and then end sharply and incisively.

· Employ your imagination, and avoid a trite ending.

• Make your ending brief: do not gyrate around until you mercifully finish.

• Employ some of the many forms of conclusion:

1. *Quotation.* A striking quotation provides a sharp ending.

2. *Summary.* A recapitulation of your main points is effective.

3. *Question.* A direct question keeps your listeners with you to the end.

4. *Appeal to Action.* A final appeal to action carries your motivation step through the conclusion and leaves your audience dynamized.

4

MAKE IT INTERESTING

A persuasive sermon requires one final quality: it must be interesting. Many preachers, unfortunately, are concerned only with making their sermon true, and give little attention to making it interesting. And this can result in a sermon that is logical and true and correct and orthodox—but boring.

If your sermon is not interesting, a major part of its effectiveness is lost. You want the people in the audience to hear your argument, but if your talk is basically dry and uninteresting they will find it difficult to pay attention. In the preceding chapter we cited two examples of lead-ins to magazine articles, the one phrased in a human interest story about a traffic fatality, the other in dry, pedantic language. Readers find their interest engaged in the first example and want to continue reading, but in the other they must force themselves to read on, as if they were reading a page from a text book. The same thing transpires in public speaking: the interesting talk engages the listener's attention and makes him want to hear what the speaker says next, while the dry and uninteresting talk becomes a chore to hear, something your listener must force himself to follow.

You cannot persuade your audience by the sheer power of your logic alone; you must make it interesting for him, too. We said that public speaking is conversation projected, but good conversation must be interesting. We would not enjoy a conversation with someone who only spouted data and statistics, threw quotation after quotation at us, and tried to overpower us by the force of his deadly logic. That is not human. We want to talk with people who are human and interesting, who are pleasant to hear, who have flavor in their conversation. This is no less true in the area of public speaking.

Hence, a principle: *The preacher must not only attempt to make his sermon true and logical, but also interesting and attractive!*

We will discuss here three fundamental ways of making your sermon interesting: illustration, word power, and emotion.

1. ILLUSTRATION.

The humanists of the late Renaissance had a phrase which they employed as their standard: "The proper study of man is man." Correctly understood, the phrase contains a fundamental truth—that people are interested in people, that people enjoy hearing about other people. For the public speaker, this has broad implications: it means that stories about people can create an instant reaction of interest from his audience.

Every audience, no matter what its caliber, enjoys an intelligent story about people. The preacher would be wise, therefore, to employ this ready access to audience interest. Jesus Himself employed this technique constantly. He related stories about people in familiar situations, and employed these stories to illustrate the vital truths He was preaching. Earlier we recommended a study of the relevancy in Christ's preaching, His ability to relate His material directly to His listeners. You might also note His use of stories to cement that relevancy and create audience interest. Recall the stories of the laborers in the vineyard, the wedding banquet, the talents buried in a field, the unmerciful servant, the good Samaritan, the prodigal son, the beggar at the gate, the corrupt judge. There is an impressive list of stories in the preaching of Jesus, and the contemporary preacher would do well to examine carefully the Lord's technique.

Jesus was able to engage the interest of His listeners through His stories, and through them He was better able to explain His doctrine and make it more intelligible. And those are the two great benefits any preacher obtains by using a story: audience interest and better communication of the truth you are preaching. Those are no small advantages!

A good story can be employed at almost any place in a sermon—in the introduction, the conclusion, in any one of the steps in the FERM principle. No matter when you relate a story, the audience will respond to it immediately. When the preacher says, "I'd like to tell you a true story about . . . ," the interest of your listeners quickens and there are few wandering minds. People love to hear about people.

A principle, then: *Relate stories in your sermon to gain immediate interest from your audience.*

Preachers frequently say, however, that they would like to use stories in their sermons, but they do not know where to find them. That is an unfortunate attitude, because good stories for sermons are all around us. We live in a world of stories about people. The preacher must become convinced of the utility of using stories as Christ did, and then he must keep his eyes and ears alert for any good story he encounters. He will find a rich harvest of stories.

The priest is, by vocation, committed to the needs of his people: He must think about them, care for them. He should extend this commitment to the preparation of his sermons and keep his people in mind as he encounters interesting and illustrative stories. "There's an interesting story," he might say to himself, "I can use that in a sermon."

He will find stories for sermons in the daily newspaper, magazines, his own encounters with people. Any good story can be used someplace in one of your sermons. One of the most intriguing of Jesus' stories is related in a sermon in the 13th chapter of St. Luke's Gospel. It reads:

> Do you think that these Galileans were worse sinners than all the other Galileans, because they suffered such things? I tell you no; but unless you repent, you will all perish in the same manner. Or those eighteen upon whom the tower of Siloe fell and killed them; do you think that they were more guilty than all the other dwellers in Jerusalem? I tell you no; but unless you repent you will all perish in the same manner.

What is all that business about the tower of Siloe? We do not know, because it was some local accident that apparently had caused a good deal of comment in Palestine. The intriguing fact is that Jesus is taking some burning news item of the day and weaving it into his sermon. He was alert for material to use in his sermons, and he gathered in this particular item for later use. We do not know if all the characters in the Lord's parables are real historical characters: the prodigal son, Lazarus, the good Samaritan, and the rest. They could have been created fictionally by the Lord, although I personally feel that they represent true historical episodes. But whether they are fictional or not, they are drawn from real life and contain realistic characterization. These are no cardboard characters the Lord is using, they are flesh and blood people. The pertinent fact for the preacher is the Lord's use of realistic stories, and His ability to draw them from the world in which we live. The contemporary preacher, if he is alert, can discover innumerable stories.

You can also find valuable stories in the vast world of history and literature. The lives of Caesar, Napoleon, Lincoln, for example, can provide a variety of illustrative incidents. And the works of Shakespeare and Dickens, to name just two authors, contain a storehouse of sharp characterizations and lively episodes. The preacher must read not merely for enjoyment, but also for the benefit of his future listeners who could profit by these anecdotes if they were used to flavor a sermon.

The Christian heroes, the saints, offer another whole rich field of stories. We have entered into a new era in hagiography in which the saints are being presented as true flesh and blood people and not mere pious statues. This is extremely advantageous for the preacher, since he can use these characterizations in his sermons. If the preacher talks about the saints as real people in real situations and does not indulge in pietisms about them, he can bring particular impact to his sermon because these heroes of God represent people who have lived the divine life completely. There is nothing pietistic, for example, about St. Vincent de Paul's climbing through the grim alleys of Paris bringing food to hungry people; or St. Thomas More's sitting in the Tower of London waiting to die; or St. Peter Claver's washing the sores of his maltreated Negroes in the Spanish colony of Cartegena; or St. Joan of Arc strapped to the stake at Rouen. The saints, described as authentic human beings, have special appeal for the Christian audience; these proven heroes of God are people who have heard the message of Christ and made it effective and dynamic in their own situations. St. Francis of Assisi shows us the happiness of belonging to God. St. John Bosco presents a picture of dedication to the instruction of youth. St. Isaac Jogues demonstrates how to love and serve even those people who mistrust our intentions. St. Louis, king of France, shows how to combine a life of intense sanctity and active political endeavor. St. Frances Xavier Cabrini presents a picture of the involved Christian who saw opportunities to spread the love of Jesus everywhere, who found the world too small for her activity.

The Scriptures also offer a treasure lode of story material that the preacher should be especially interested in using. The life of Jesus, His episodes, His encounters with people, His career, His dialogue —all present the most moving of illustrative material. Nor should the preacher neglect the Old Testament, which is a veritable library of human drama and biography. The figures of the pre-Christian era are vivid and colorful personalities, and they demonstrate in their lives important lessons that God is teaching us through them. Abraham presents a splendid picture of the obedient servant of God. Job shows us trust in God. David, the figure of true repentance. Solomon, the picture of a good man disintegrating. Judith, a study in female courage. Jonathan, true friendship. Jephte, fidelity to commitment. Josue, courage and fearlessness for the Lord. The list is interminable.

Stories from life, from contemporary news, from history, from literature, from hagiography, from Scripture. How can the preacher say he does not know where to discover stories and illustrations for his sermons? The stories are there, but the preacher must be alert, he must keep his antennae up.

It is advisable for the preacher to maintain his own reference file of stories. We often encounter impressive stories that would be excellent material for a sermon, but because we do not make a note of them we are unable to recall them at the moment of sermon composition. Only a minimal amount of effort is required to record a story, but it can be immensely rewarding for the preacher. A story recorded here, and another one there, soon add up to an invaluable reference file of illustrative material. The preacher should record *any* good story he discovers (whether it be from the world of news, or sports, or books) because any story that is human and moving can be used effectively sometime in a sermon.

People love to hear about people, and the injection of intelligent and human stories in your sermon can attract unusual audience interest. Therefore, keep your antennae up for good material. It is all around you.

2. WORD POWER.

Your sermon can be made attractive and interesting by selecting the right words in which to clothe your ideas. The preacher should exercise special effort to select his words carefully because he, unlike other public speakers, is handicapped by an ecclesiastical vocabulary which is dull and uninteresting and platitudinous. At the outset, the preacher should attempt to expurgate the whole vocabulary of ecclesiastical clichés from his language and substitute more simple and meaningful words. Here are some of the terrible words and phrases that preachers inflict on their listeners:

> voluntary acts
> ignominious death on the cross
> intrinsic
> prone to take
> requisite dispositions
> efficacious acts
> the divine attributes
> valid but not licit
> the ineffable mystery
> recourse to prayer
> inordinate desires
> satisfy the divine justice
> open the gates of heaven
> under pain of mortal sin
> incur the wrath of God
> corporal works
> an act of your will
> purity of intention
> temporal blessings
> the economy of our salvation

This painful list could be extended indefinitely, but a further compilation would only be as wearisome to read as it is tedious to hear. This kind of ecclesiastical vocabulary is not a bright, fresh, statement of God's revelation, but only a tired mixture of text book theology, scholastic philosophy and Roman law—and the net result is a body of clichés that numbs the attention of the audience.

The preacher, who is necessarily committed to a communication art, should become conscious of the power of words. He should recognize that something that is stated in direct, meaningful, fresh language can have impact on his audience, while something that is stated in words similar to the horrible clichés we cited above can only paralyze his listeners.

This does not imply that the preacher needs to pepper his sermon with a large and erudite vocabulary; it merely means that he must use the intelligible words of human communication, and not the pedantic and technical phrases that creep into the preacher's vocabulary. Great and impressive pronouncements are often made with a simple, human vocabulary. For example, Lincoln in his Second Inaugural stated:

> With malice toward none, with charity for all, with firmness in the right as God gives us to see the right, let us strive on to finish the work we are in.

Or John Kennedy in his Inaugural:

> In the long history of the world, only a few generations have been granted the role of defending freedom in its hour of maximum danger. I do not shrink from this responsibility—I welcome it. I do not believe that any of us would exchange places with any other people or any other generation. The energy, the faith, the devotion which we bring to this endeavor will light our country and all who serve it—and the glow from that fire can truly light the world.

These are powerful and moving statements, but you will notice that the words used are simple ones, all within the range of the average person's vocabulary. But both statements demonstrate a clear consciousness of the power of words. The words are sharp, clear, arranged for impact and meaning. There is no use of anything like "efficacious acts" or "requisite dispositions" or "ineffable mystery."

A basic and urgent rule for the preacher is: *Throw away your dry and technical vocabulary, and use the fresh simple words of human communication.*

In selecting his vocabulary, the preacher should make an effort to employ those stronger and sharper words of Anglo-Saxon origin, rather than the weaker and softer words of Latin origin. Words like *run, jump, hit, laugh* are of Anglo-Saxon root, and they have greater impact than Latin transliterations like *predestined, circumscribe, designate.* This does not imply that words of Latin origin should never be employed, but it does mean that the Anglo-Saxon words should be in the majority. Reread the Lincoln and Kennedy statements above and you will notice the preference for the words of Anglo-Saxon root.

And develop a feeling and sensitivity for using words that have appeal for your listeners. Wilfred Funk, the lexicographer, has compiled a list of what he considers the ten most beautiful words in the

English language. Funk's list should make intriguing reading for the public speaker:

> Dawn, hush, lullaby, murmuring, tranquil, mist,
> luminous, chimes, golden, melody.

Read that list slowly, lingering over the words, and you will feel the impact that words can make and almost see the images they conjure. You can create a whole atmosphere by the words you employ, and you can sometimes say more with a few carefully selected words than with whole paragraphs of intense logic.

Words are the speaker's tools: use them wisely and they will add verve and color to the ideas you are trying to express: use them poorly and you will appear clumsy and heavy handed, a man who does not really know how to use his native idiom.

An examination of Jesus' preaching will reveal His concern for the selection of the right word and phrase, and His appreciation for the power of words. He employed metaphors, similes, sharp imagery, comparisons, figures of speech—a broad array of careful word selection designed to engage and interest His listeners. Recall some of His phrases:

> No one pours new wine in old wine skins.

> If a house is divided against itself, that house cannot stand.

> It is not the healthy who need a physician, but the sick.

> No one can enter the strong man's house and plunder his goods unless he first binds the strong man.

> You are the salt of the earth. Suppose salt become insipid; how can you restore its tang?

> The kingdom of heaven is like leaven which a woman took and buried in three measures of flour until all of it was leavened.

> Men do not light a lamp and then put it under a bushel basket. They set it on a stand where it gives light to all in the house.

> Now from the fig tree learn this parable. When its branch is now tender, and the leaves break forth, you know that summer is near.

The eye is the lamp of the body. If your eye is sound your whole body will be full of light.

By their fruits you will know them. Do men gather grapes from thorns, or figs from thistles?

Be wise as serpents and guileless as doves.

Woe to you, Scribes and Pharisees. Hypocrites! Because you are like whitened sepulchres, which outwardly appear to be beautiful, but within are full of dead men's bones and all uncleanness.

How often would I have gathered your children together, as a hen gathers her young under her wings.

There is evident in the preaching of Jesus a determined program to use colorful speech, as the above excerpts from his sermons demonstrate. The Lord had a striking awareness of the power of words and He chose them carefully and effectively, using figures of speech to gain the greatest impact on His audience. New wine and salt and a physician and a bushel basket and a fig tree and a strong man—this is good language, bright and vigorous, far removed from dull phrases like "efficacious acts" and "requisite dispositions."

Jesus employed a simple vocabulary, but He had a great respect for the power of words. They were for Him tools to be used in public speaking, techniques for communication, means for creating audience interest. If the contemporary preacher wants to interest his audience he must learn the Lord's lesson—throw away your platitudes, become conscious of the power of words, use them carefully in bright and vigorous speech patterns!

3. EMOTION.

Preachers often think that there is something suspect or unworthy in an appeal to emotion during a sermon. Religion is not an emotional thing, they say, it is a rational approach to God based on a response to His revelation. True enough, but it does not follow that man's emotions must be divorced from religion, that the Church will take care of man's intellect and will and then allow his emotions to be engaged wherever else he will. God wants the whole man —mind, heart, *and* emotions. And an appeal to emotion in a sermon, provided a proper appeal has been made to his intellect, is legitimate, effective, and sometimes necessary.

Jesus Himself frequently made an appeal to His listener's emotions and thereby engaged the entire man in his message. He made His listeners *feel* as well as *understand*, and His argument became overwhelming. The story of the prodigal son is a case in point. The parable mounts in emotional impact as the tale unfolds: the son demanding his inheritance, his rejection of the family, his journey into a far country, his profligate squandering of the money, his fallen state, his misery, his recollection of his father's goodness, the journey home, the father viewing him from a distance—and then in an unforgettable scene, the father rushes down the hill, embraces and kisses his son, while the son sobs his sorrow and the father cries out, "Fetch quickly the best robe and put it on him, and give him a ring for his finger and sandals for his feet, and bring out the fatted calf and kill it, and let us eat and make merry, because this son of mine was dead and has come back to life again; he was lost, and has been found." The emotional effect on Christ's audience must have been stunning. The Lord had led them through this appealing parable, involving their emotions in a story of a boy who deserted his family, and as Jesus carried the story through to its climax He finished in a mighty crescendo, painting the picture of the sobbing son and the father shouting to the servants to make ready a great feast. Jesus had effectively communicated His message: He was speaking about God's mercy, and then He drove home His point by this emotion-packed story which made His listeners understand and feel the reality of God's mercy.

The parable of the good Samaritan is another of the many occasions when He made an emotional appeal to His audience. The story was in response to the question, "Who is my neighbor?" The Lord paints a scene of the man who was beaten and stripped and left seriously wounded by a group of thieves, and then He introduces two characters who pass the wounded man lying bleeding in the road. The priest sees him and hurries past. And a Levite also walks hurriedly past the fallen man. The Lord makes a point of stating that both travelers *saw* the man in the road. Then a Samaritan, a foreigner despised by the Jews, stops and ministers to the man, lifts him on his beast and carries him to an inn. When the Samaritan leaves the next day he offers money to the innkeeper: "Take care of him, and whatever more you spend, I will repay you on my return." Jesus had involved His listeners in the plight of the wounded man, and then depicted the two Jews, who should have helped the man, hurrying past. But this Samaritan, for whom the Jews had little respect, performs the act of kindness. The Lord had induced disgust for the two Jews, and chagrin and surprise that the despised foreigner should do the right thing. In fact, when Jesus asked His listeners to tell Him who had proved himself a true neighbor, they could not even say the Samaritan's name—only "He who took pity on him." Jesus had evoked His listeners' emotions and showed them graphically that the person who exercises charity is the true friend of God, no matter what be his race or nationality. He had completely involved His listeners in His message.

The appeal to emotion can be occasionally employed with great effectiveness by the contemporary preacher, but he should bear in mind two fundamental rules about employing emotion in a sermon:

1. The appeal to emotion should be genuine, not artificial. It was Oscar Wilde who said that no man of feeling could read the death of Little Nell in Dickens without laughing. The implication here is that an honest emotion must be evoked through honest means and not by mere sentimentality. The saccharin words, the roseate story, the effete mood—all these are an appeal to sentimentality, not honest emotion. In the parable of the prodigal son, Jesus made His listeners feel confidence in God's mercy through the emotional impact of the father's reception of his profligate son; and in the parable of the good Samaritan, he made them feel shame and surprise that they did not recognize the true demands of serving God. These are genuine emotions, and Jesus evoked them in an honest way, not through a sentimental approach.

The modern preacher could make his audience feel love for God, detestation for sin, desire for heaven, compassion for our brothers. There is nothing ersatz about these emotions.

2. Emotion is based on truth. We can induce the most intense emotional reaction in a talk by being as realistic as possible. The real engages our emotions the most effectively: for example, a silent newsreel film about victims staggering from the atomic blast at Hiroshima engages our shock, our sympathy, our compassion. It is realistic, it is true, and it involves us quickly.

A contemporary preacher could, for example, relate the story of Kitty Genovese, the girl who was killed in New York while a number of people witnessed her attack from their windows and refused to help her. The preacher's point could be the serious obligation we have to help those who need us, and a simple narration of the Genovese story could have great emotional impact on an audience. The factual nature of the story increases the emotional content.

The preacher, therefore, does not have to reach far to contrive some emotional impact. It is gathered from life—from the story of the prodigal son, the good Samaritan, Kitty Genovese. Hearts and flowers do not generate true emotion, but realistic portrayals of life do, those stories and facts that are torn from the raw stuff of life, that quickly engage our emotions of love and shame and disgust and compassion.

Do not be afraid to make an appeal to emotion—you are making an appeal to the whole man. The appeal to reason must, of course, be included someplace in your sermon, but if you evoke a genuine emotion and base it on realism you are presenting a total argument that your listener cannot deny.

———

Illustration. Word power. Emotion. These are the three avenues to quick audience interest. The use of stories, a careful selection of words, and an occasional appeal to emotion can lift your sermon out of the area of the dull lecture and into the appealing area of the interesting talk. The average listener will not give you sustained attention if you only throw fact after fact at him. He wants to be addressed as a human being. That is the way Jesus addressed His audiences.

As the preacher studies the material for his sermon, he should ask himself the probing question: "It is true and logical, but is it *interesting?*"

EXERCISES

Remember the principle: You must not only attempt to make your sermon true and logical, but also interesting and attractive!

1. *Illustration.*
   - Relate stories in your sermon to gain immediate interest from your audience.
   - Study Jesus' technique in using stories.
   - Keep your antennae up—good stories are all around you:
     - In newspapers and periodicals and your own encounters with people. (Remember the tower of Siloe.)
     - In the world of history and literature.

• In the lives of the saints. (But relate human and realistic stories, not pietistic ones.)

• In the Scriptures: the life of Jesus, and the stories of those vivid and colorful personalities in the Old Testament.

• Maintain a reference file of stories. Record any good story you discover; you can use it someplace in a sermon.

2. *Word Power.*

• Throw away your dry and technical vocabulary, and use the fresh simple words of human communication.

• Reread the list of ecclesiastical clichés in this chapter, and ascertain if they constitute a large part of your public speaking vocabulary.

• Reread the excerpts from the Lincoln and Kennedy addresses, and note the impact that simple words can have if they are used carefully.

• Use the strong words of Anglo-Saxon origin in preference to the weaker transliterations from the Latin.

• Develop a feeling and a sensitivity for the power of words.

• Study Jesus' technique in using colorful language—figures of speech, metaphors, similes, imagery, comparisons.

• Remember: Bright and attractive words engage the attention of your listener, while dry and abstract and technical language paralyzes him.

3. *Emotion.*

• Do not be afraid to make an appeal to emotion: It is valuable to make your listener *feel* as well as *understand.*

• Study Jesus' technique in employing the appeal to emotion.

• Your appeal to emotion should be genuine, not artificial: Do not appeal to sentimentality or an ersatz emotion.

• The most impressive emotional appeal is based on realism, facts torn from the real stuff of life.

5

CONSTRUCTING YOUR OUTLINE

A sermon, as we indicated in Part I, demands preparation. Ideas must be collected and organized, a thesis developed, phraseology worked out, stories assembled for possible use, introduction and conclusion prepared. All of this requires preparation on the part of the speaker; it cannot be done off the top of the head when the man is at the lectern. The preacher has to force himself to the hard business of taking pencil in hand and working it out on paper.

It is not advisable for the speaker of any experience to write every word of his sermon, then memorize it and recite it to the audience exactly as written. That type of presentation is too flat and dull; it destroys the electricity and excitement of direct audience contact because the speaker must be working inside himself trying to recall his written words and phrases in their precise order. The memorized sermon—or the *declamation*, as it is called—is treacherous: If the speaker who has memorized his talk word by word forgets a word or phrase, the whole structure might come apart and he will be unable to continue. Furthermore, the memorized talk is impractical for the preacher who is doing any sizeable amount of public speaking: One man in our contemporary society simply cannot find the time to write every sermon completely and then memorize the entire manuscript.

It is perhaps advisable for the novice speaker to write and memorize his sermons in their entirety until he gains a little experience in the pulpit. Initial pulpit experiences are a bit frightening, and until the preacher learns to compose himself before an audience it might be prudent if he has memorized words to fall back upon. But, after a short while, when he has his composure and has acquired some amount of fluency before an audience, he should begin to speak from outline. That is the natural, effective, practical way to speak in public.

However, the outline a preacher composes to prepare himself for a sermon must be a full, detailed outline, not merely a few sentences hurriedly put together. The outline might consist of a number of pages: the key ideas, subdivisions, illustrations, introduction and conclusion. The preacher should work over this outline, making it as complete as possible. Then when he has organized his outline satisfactorily, he should commit its basic structure to memory and speak from this in the pulpit. He will have the advantage of an organized, well-planned talk that he can give with all the spontaneity, all the dynamism, all the naturalness the preaching experience demands.

The process of preparing an outline can be reduced to a four-step procedure.

1. ASSEMBLE YOUR IDEAS.
2. SELECT YOUR IDEAS.
3. WRITE YOUR OUTLINE.
4. REVIEW YOUR OUTLINE.

1. ASSEMBLE YOUR IDEAS.

After the preacher has selected his topic, he should begin to gather ideas for his sermon based on that topic. A most serviceable technique is to take a piece of paper and write all the ideas you can recall about the topic, without regard to order or sequence or even possible use in the sermon. This is called "brainstorming," and it helps to get the mental processes started. You know that you will have to develop the FERM principle, so you can write whatever facts you can recall, the explanation of those facts, the relevancy of them, and the motivation. But brainstorming should not be limited to that; it should gather anything relating to the topic—stories, definitions, quotations, anything at all.

Research is also part of the assembly of ideas. Consult books. Get the scriptural references. Look for illustrations. Study the explanations of your topic. And put all this on your paper.

As yet you have only an unorganized mass of material. That is fine: you are merely trying to assemble ideas. It is extremely valuable if a number of days can elapse between this step and the following ones: Then you will discover that more ideas will appear, that your original ideas will germinate other ideas. If you can arrange this time interval, place your paper in an available place on your desk, and jot down ideas as they come to you. Continue to think about your sermon at odd moments, and new ideas will come to you. You might discover that you have compiled two or three pages of unorganized notes.

2. SELECT YOUR IDEAS.

In the next step, you select a thesis that you want to develop in the sermon, and then you must personalize that thesis. From your pages of notes, you will want to choose those elements that fit into your thesis, and this means that you will discard a lot of the material you have brainstormed. One of the problems that besets many speakers, particularly the novice, is lack of selectivity, the failure to limit the topic and thesis to practical proportions. A preacher, for example, may want to discuss the Eucharist, and he will try to tell the whole story in a short sermon—the Old Testament analogies, the promise of Jesus, the institution, an explanation of the Mass, and practical advice for reception of the Eucharist. That is too much: it is unwieldy and unmanageable, and ultimately confusing to the audience. The speaker should limit his topic, take one phase of the question, and develop that adequately.

When you complete this step you will have indicated on your notes those ideas you want to include in your sermon.

3. WRITE YOUR OUTLINE.

On a fresh piece of paper, the speaker should then develop his ideas according to the FERM principle: facts, explanation, relevancy, and motivation. These are the elements that must be included in your sermon to achieve persuasiveness. You should add illustrations and take care that your language is fresh and vigorous and free of platitudes.

Write the key ideas in schematic form, then add sentences under each key point to develop that idea. You are not writing each word you will say in the pulpit, only a schematic outline.

You can write your introduction and conclusion after you have completed the body of the talk. It is extremely advisable to write out these two parts completely, the only two parts you will compose in their entirety, because they must be sharp and precise. You cannot afford to fumble your introduction or conclusion.

The outline must, of course, be written to fit the allotted time span of the sermon. On some occasions a determined amount of time is allotted and expected, while on other occasions the length of the talk is left to the speaker's discretion. As a general principle, it is far better to speak for too short a time rather than speak at too great a length. The attention span of the modern audience, which is accustomed to a rapid pace of life and instant change, is a short one. People find it difficult to sustain their attention through a long talk, unless it is particularly interesting and engaging. Thus a seven or eight minute sermon can often be more effective than a fifteen minute one—it is more precise, more incisive, more easily followed by the audience. The old Latin axiom has it: *Qui nimis probat, nihil probat* (He who proves too much, proves nothing). The speaker must be sure that there is no padding on his talk, no circumlocution, no meandering. It should be lean and tight, immediate and directly to the point. If the speaker has any doubt about whether or not he should include some material, or whether perhaps it is superfluous, then leave it out.

One vital point: You are not outlining an essay; you are outlining something to be spoken. Therefore you must continually test your words and phrases for the area of the spoken word. State your phrases aloud, if necessary. But do not become so involved in your paper that you begin to compose an essay. Ask yourself how it sounds, not how it reads. This requires a more subtle judgment than you would make if you were outlining an essay: In the essay you are making a judgment about the readable character of what you have written, but here you are making a judgment about its audible character. You are doing something a musical composer does when he writes a song: he thinks of an arrangement of notes in his mind, and then he plays it on his piano with a few fingers to see how it sounds. The speaker must be continually listening, with his inner ear, to ascertain how his outline sounds. The speaker's rule of thumb should be: *Play it on the piano to see how it sounds!*

4. REVIEW YOUR OUTLINE.

When you have completed your outline, you should begin to review it and study it in preparation for your appearance in the pulpit. The key divisions should be firmly committed to memory so that you will be able to deliver the main line of your argument without hesitancy. This fundamental framework must be retained in your mind, so that even if you forget some of the subdivisions under your key idea you can continue on to the next main point without any interruption of the fluency of the sermon.

As you review your outline, you perhaps might add an idea or two, change the construction of some phrase, insert another story. This is part of the process that takes place as you approach the moment of your appearance in the pulpit. The excitement of public speaking should be growing within you. Soon you will step into the pulpit and have the opportunity of communicating the important truths you have prepared. You are motivated, you are audience-related, you have prepared your sermon. You are ready.

Do not carry notes or outline into the pulpit with you. This erects a barrier between the speaker and his audience: The speaker is conscious of his notes and his attention is constantly being directed toward them. If you have prepared yourself adequately there is no need for any memoranda in the pulpit. You have assembled your ideas, written them into an outline, committed the broad structure of that outline to memory—now speak to your audience!

In summary: You must prepare yourself for your sermon, and this is accomplished through a four-step process—assemble your ideas, select your ideas, write your outline, review your outline. If you do that, you are ready for your audience.

EXERCISES

Remember: The sermon from outline is the most effective and practical way to speak.

Construct your outline in the four-step procedure:

1. *Assemble your ideas.*
   - Brainstorm your topic, writing down all the ideas you can gather about your subject.
   - Research your topic: read, consult, search.
   - Attempt to allow a time interval between this step and the following ones so that your original ideas will germinate other ideas.

2. *Select your ideas.*
   - Select your thesis. Personalize it.
   - From your mass of unorganized material choose those ideas and illustrations and phrases that fit your thesis.
   - Limit your material to practical proportions.

3. *Write your outline.*
  · Develop your thesis according to the FERM principle.
  · Use fresh and vigorous language. Avoid clichés and plati-tudes.
  · Write your outlines schematically: key ideas, and then the development of those ideas in subdivisions.
  · Write your introduction and conclusion in their entirety.
  · As a general principle, it is far better to speak for too short a time rather than speak at too great a length. Your audience has a short attention span. Thus if you have any doubt, leave it out.
  · Compose your outline for the *spoken* word, asking yourself how it sounds, not how it reads. Play it on the piano to see how it sounds.

4. *Review your outline.*
  · Review and study your written outline in preparation for your appearance in the pulpit.
  · Commit the principal divisions of the sermon firmly to memory.
  · Do not carry the outline to the pulpit: speak directly and immediately to your listeners, following the structure of your outline.

· Review the exercises of the Art of Persuasion: the speaker's goal of persuasion; the FERM principle; introductions and conclusions; making it interesting.
· Review the Art of Public Speaking: the speaker's mentality; the ASRM principle; and the conversational mode.
· Coordinate the whole procedure: it will produce a poised speaker giving a persuasive and interesting talk.

III

THE ART OF PREACHING

1

THE GOOD NEWS

St. Mark says in his Gospel that Jesus journeyed through Palestine "heralding the good news of God's kingdom." Every Christian preacher is called to imitate and perpetuate Jesus' preaching: to herald the joyful tidings of God's kingdom, to announce the good news that God has come, that He loves us, that He is our way and our truth and our life. That is the preacher's fundamental mission.

However, as we indicated previously, the Christian preacher has not always been faithful to that mission, and there has been a disheartening decline in the vigor and quality of Catholic preaching during the past four centuries. A number of things went wrong. Less attention was paid to the basic "good news" of Jesus' preaching, and more attention was given to derivative sources: St. Alphonsus was employed more than St. Paul, and St. Francis de Sales was quoted more than St. Luke. Unfriendly currents of thought made their inroads into the preacher's message: Jansenism, which expounded a hostility and distrust for human nature; Pelagianism, which placed more emphasis on man's spiritual accomplishments than on God's redeeming love; illuminism, which turned its attention to a future destiny and ignored the real world in which we live. Some preachers separated the moral content from the total Christian message, and only spoke of the sins that could be committed with the result that their preaching degenerated into owlish moralizing. Others became dire prophets of doom and preached thundering sermons about a vengeful God, describing the vivid fires of hell and its sulphurous fumes. And others allowed their preaching to descend into a sickly sentimentality in which God is so good and everything is so beautiful and there are no real problems.

The preacher became less and less interested in preaching, and he therefore became less and less a herald of the joyful tidings of God's kingdom. He was a servant of God, a minister of the sacraments, a good man—but not a herald of Christ. The distinguished Protestant theologian Karl Barth describes the situation:

> The Catholic Church eschews the personal, dynamic, faith-evoking ministry of the word out of preference for the static, automatic and even "magical" ministry of the sacrament, so that the Catholic Church may rightly be called a Church of the Sacrament and Protestantism a Church of the Living Word.

Whether Barth's statement be completely accurate or not, it does point to a real problem: That Catholic preachers have, to some extent, neglected their responsibility to preach the word.

The revival in Catholic preaching sponsored by Vatican II seeks to eliminate the misdirections preaching has taken and to return to a vital, dynamic preaching of the gospel. This preaching is being called *kerygmatic*, an excellent word, but one that requires explanation. The Greek word *kerygma* is used seven times in the New Testament, and it means literally a herald's proclamation of an important truth. In context in the New Testament it refers to the basic content of the apostolic preaching. The corresponding Greek verb *kerysso* (to herald an important truth) is used sixty-one times in the New Testament and refers to the herald's action in announcing the truth and calling his listeners to action. It is applied directly to the preaching of Jesus in three texts, one of which is used in the opening sentence of this chapter. (Mark 1, 14)

Kerygma, therefore, is the scriptural word used to describe Christian preaching, and as such it deserves our most careful attention.* The one word *kerygma* embraces two concepts: the proclamation of the truth and the truth itself. And there you have the essence of

---

* Many authors also cite another scriptural word *didache* as a further form of Christian teaching. They claim that *didache* (teaching) as used in the Epistles connotes a more advanced form of teaching for the initiate, while *kerygma* pertains chiefly to preaching to unbelievers. Such a distinction, however, seems unnecessary and unfounded. Cf. *Paul On Preaching* by Murphy-O'Connor (New York, 1964), pp. 67–71; and *The Art of Teaching Christian Doctrine* by Hofinger (Notre Dame, 1957), p. 6. The *kerygma* appears to include all forms of public Christian preaching—at least, that is the sense it is used in modern kerygmatics; and that, of course, is the sense in which this book uses it.

kerygmatic preaching—it describes a specific kind of preacher and a specific kind of message.

The preacher is to be the *keryx*, the herald—the enthusiastic, vital, dynamic speaker who engages the attention of his listeners and makes them pay attention to the things he is saying, and then prods his listeners into action.

The message is the basic content of Jesus' revelation, the good news (Greek: *euaggelion*) that Christ proclaimed in the scriptures.

Joining the two concepts, then, we arrive at an understanding of kerygmatic preaching, the kind of preaching the Church wants its preachers to practice: *The kerygmatic preacher is one who preaches the good news enthusiastically.*

Whenever Christian preaching has been deficient, it was precisely because it was not kerygmatic. When the preacher was not a *keryx*, a herald, he tended to become a catechist or a moralist or an indifferent prattler of ecclesiastical platitudes. And when the preacher was not preaching the good news, he descended into Jansenism or Pelagianism or illuminism or moralisms or terrorisms or sentimentality.

In the first two sections of this book—The Art of Public Speaking and The Art of Persuasion—we discussed the preacher's role as herald; the dynamic, vital, enthusiastic speaker who communicates with his listeners in language they can understand. In this final section of the book, The Art of Preaching, we will sketch the broad outlines of the herald's message: the essential *kerygma*, the good news, the revelation of Jesus. It is this *kerygma* that the priest should preach, and when he deserts it for something else, he is unfaithful to the mission Jesus has given him.

The preacher needs to subject himself to a personal searching analysis about the content of his preaching. Is he preaching the good news of the kingdom, or is he preaching something else? Has he perhaps allowed his preaching to become a mixture of popular psychology and derivative Christian authors and homey maxims, all flavored with a few texts from the scriptures? Is he moralizing in the pulpit, limiting the dynamic Christian message to a repetitious series of thou-shall and thou-shall-not? Is he preaching pie-in-the-sky, asking his audience to huddle in the sacristy with him reciting prayers and avoiding any realistic Christian engagement with life? Has he reduced the broad sweep of the Christian life to a number of pious devotions and nervous religious exercises? Is he a Cotton Mather in the pulpit, constantly shouting fearsome threats about damnation and destruction and hell's fires? Is he sentimentalizing about religion, describing it as a saccharin composite of holy pictures, flickering candles, and artless statues? Is he platitudinous, solving all of life's real problems with a few quick clichés and tired axioms?

If he is doing any of these things, he is not preaching the good news, he is not an authentic herald of Christ, and he must reexamine the message of Jesus. The Lord's preaching was a stirring joyous body of truths bearing little resemblance to that strange mixture of deviations and half-truths.

The basic kerygma of Jesus can be summarized under five headings: Incarnational, Religious, Moral, Social, and Eschatalogical. Here is a brief synopsis of the good news:

1. *Incarnational.*
The eternal God, the Trinity from on high, has through the ages manifested Himself to us, demonstrating His power and His timeless love for us; and in the fullness of time Jesus, the Son of God, became man and offered us His love and His salvation, and His mercy. We must believe in Him; we must respond to Him.

2. *Religious.*
Jesus elevates us to a new plane of existence, the life of grace, in which we are adopted into an intimate friendship with God, experiencing Him as someone to know and someone to love. We are to love Him in our hearts, associating with Him joyfully in friendship, worshiping Him in spirit and truth, but we are also to worship Him communally in union with our brothers at the eucharistic sacrifice, which is the continuing act of His redemptive love for us. And through the sacramental system Jesus sustains us in our friendship with Him, providing His love and His help and His grace at every pivotal moment of our lives.

3. *Moral.*
Jesus reaffirms the eternal law of God, the commandments, and adds a new commandment that "you love one another as I love you." He charges us to respect the sanctity of the individual, the holiness of marriage, and the good of society. We must avoid sin because of Him: "If you love Me, keep My commandments."

4. *Social.*

Jesus incorporates us into the kingdom of God, a vital union with our brothers that begins on this earth and reaches final fulfillment in the kingdom of heaven. We are to be involved with our brothers, sharing their joys and their needs, extending our realistic love to every human being.

5. *Eschatalogical.*

Jesus is risen and reigning and loving, and His Easter victory is our victory, the final act of our salvation. Through baptism our resurrection has already begun, and we are voyagers on the way to sharing Jesus' resurrection. This is the secret of the Christian's gigantic joy. But if we reject the love of Jesus and His promise of resurrection, we condemn ourselves to the eternal torment of losing Him.

This is the basic outline of good news that Jesus preached and the essential content of kerygmatic preaching. This is the message that the Christian preacher must announce to his audience, expressing it in contemporary idiom and relating it to the real situation of his listeners. If the preacher does not base the general theme of his preaching on this *kerygma* he is teaching a doctrine that—whatever it might be called—is certainly not the good news of Jesus Christ.

One caution concerning a possible misunderstanding about kerygmatic preaching: Kerygmatic preaching is not a new, esoteric form of preaching, but a return to the direct, uncluttered message of Jesus. There is danger that some preachers might misunderstand this and allow their preaching to become esoteric, self-conscious, and artificial. Jesus preached the objective truths we outlined above, but He related them directly to His immediate audience. Johannes Hofinger, S.J., an outstanding exponent of kerygmatics, writes about this danger:

> A kerygmatic formation should, then, not only consider divine revelation in itself, but also take into consideration its special relevance to the mentality of the people who are to receive it today. If we cannot show that our message answers the problems that weigh on people today, how can we be surprised at the fact that they take no interest at all?

Nor should kerygmatic preaching find it necessary to devise a new vocabulary for itself. Jesus preached the objective truths in language understandable to his listeners: He talked about farmers and coins and shepherds and salt and physicians and bushel baskets. He did not employ a recondite, esoteric vocabulary. Contemporary preachers could possibly feel obliged to employ a new and somewhat stilted language in their sermons (words like: encounter, dialogue, Christ-event, triumphalism); but this would ultimately divorce the preacher from his listeners and make his message appear a private and technical thing. In fact, this language could quickly become as platitudinous as the platitudes it is trying to replace.

The point here is that the contemporary preacher should preach the basic good news of Jesus, but he should employ all the principles we outlined in The Art of Persuasion—persuasiveness, relevancy to the audience, use of illustrations and human, colorful vocabulary. That is the way Jesus preached.

Let us now examine the five basic divisions of the *kerygma* in more detail, and indicate some sermon themes that should be preached about this basic material.

1. INCARNATIONAL.

The long chronicle of salvation history is a developing, unfolding revelation that God is real and that He loves us—loves us to the extent that He is vitally interested in every detail of our lives and wants to save us.

Jesus presents God to us as a Father. A fundamental sermon of the good news, then, should be on the Fatherhood of God. Christ tells us to approach God as a Father, pray to Him as a Father, love Him with the same tenderness, the same trust, the same closeness with which we love our natural fathers. Jesus asks us to use the analogy of a natural father's love for his child and a child's love for his father as a means for understanding our relationship with God. This is a key point in the Lord's teaching: That God is real and lovable and that religion is fundamentally an experience of God. Religion is not fundamentally moral living, or ritual, or acts of human goodness (although it includes all those elements), but it is essentially a relationship with God, a union of love with Him. The preacher's task, therefore, is to show God as real and to show how we can realistically love Him—by getting to know Him through the pages of scripture, by experiencing Him in prayer, by centering our lives around Him.

The preacher could profitably speak about what the love of God really is, because the phrase is often a mere verbalism, often a cliché, for many Christians. Love proceeds through four phases: the discovery of a value-person; reverence for that person; a service of that person; and a union with that person. Our love for the Father should proceed through the same phases: recognition of His value— His goodness, His lovableness; reverence for the Father as someone unique and fascinating; service of the Father, obeying His commands; union with Him through prayer, through a coordination of our wishes with His.

Trust in God. In the sermon on the mount, Jesus relates the Father's infinite and painstaking concern for us—more than the birds of the air and the lilies of the fields; in fact, God has numbered the very hairs of our heads. We must place our trust in Him, therefore, that He will take care of us, that we are not committed to the uncertainties of a blind destiny, that He controls events. And we must trust Him even in the aching sorrows of life, as did the ancient Job: "Even though He slays me, I will still trust in Him."

Salvation. The incarnation of Jesus is the ultimate proof of God's love for us: Jesus becomes one of us, He dies on the cross to save us. The concept of salvation must, accordingly, be explained. Salvation is sharing in the resurrection of Jesus; and through baptism the Lord has begun our resurrection. Jesus *saves* us—but what does He save us from? From ourselves, of course. He restores us to a divine intimacy, He gives design to our lives, and He brings us to the resurrection. During the course of our lives we are continually encountering means for our salvation, ways to make ourselves real persons (popular expressions: "my work is my salvation," "my hobby is my salvation," "my family is my salvation"). But only Jesus offers us complete salvation, only Jesus gives us the opportunity to become a whole person with Him.

The mercy of God. Jesus shows us God as the merciful Father. He describes the mercy of God in His parables: the good shepherd, the prodigal son. And he demonstrates God's mercy in his own life: with the woman at the well in Samaria, with the woman apprehended in sin at Jerusalem, with the woman who washed His feet, with His forgiveness of Peter. God is unbelievably merciful to us, no matter what our sin, and the invitation of Jesus is a summons of return to the merciful Father.

Faith. Jesus asks us to have faith in Him, and the Christian's

whole life must be guided by that faith. Religious faith, however, is
not a blind leap in the dark, a desperate desire that it all be true.
Faith is a reasoned belief in Jesus. He announces Himself as the Son
of God, and then He proves to us irrefutably that He is what He
claims. He does things only God could do or allow: the miracles of
Jesus (healing of the lame, restoration of sight, raising from the
dead); His prophecies (about events, and His own death and resurrection); and finally the resurrection itself, when He was killed,
pierced, buried, guarded, and then rose from the dead, and ate, was
seen, was touched. We must believe what this Jesus says. We believe the things He tells us, but we do not necessarily *understand*
everything about them. Faith, then, is believing in Jesus, Who could
not possibly deceive us.

2. RELIGIOUS.

Jesus redeems us not merely by some action that is external to
our own being, by some kind of insignia that testifies that we belong
to Him; He redeems us in the innermost core of our being, He elevates us to a new plane of existence by which we become adopted
sons of God and are able to begin a life of intimate association with
Him.

Union. Jesus invites us to a life of close union with Him, asking us
to be joined with Him as closely as branches are linked to a vine.
"I call you now, not servants, but friends," He says. And: "Abide in
My love." The preacher must speak about our union with Jesus. He
must present Jesus as someone to know and someone to love. Many
Christians only know *about* Jesus, they do not know Jesus directly
and immediately as a person, someone they love and someone with
whom they are united. The preacher needs to tell his listeners
that Jesus is their intimate friend, their enduring companion, their
hope, their strength, their love. "Christ is your life," St. John says.
And St. Paul expresses what should be the true condition of every
Christian: "I live, now not I, but Christ lives in me."

Prayer. Union with the Lord demands association and companionship, and we accomplish this through prayer, our contact with
Jesus. Prayer is companionship and conversation with the Lord, and
is principally a thing of the heart, achieved in our person-to-person
experience with God. Jesus says: "But when you pray go into your
room and, closing your door, pray to your Father in secret, and your
Father, who sees in secret, will reward you. But in praying do not

multiply words, as the Gentiles do; for they think that by saying a great deal, they will be heard." Prayer of petition, of asking, is only one kind of prayer, and not the most important kind, at that. In the *Our Father* Jesus constructs the proper order of prayer: first, loving engagement with the Lord, concern for the reverence due Him, the extension of His kingdom, the accomplishment of His will; then, a filial plea for help, a petition for forgiveness of faults, concern for our brothers, and a final request for salvation. These are the things we should discuss with the Lord in prayer.

The Eucharist. Christianity, though, is not a personalistic philosophy—God alone and I, and let the rest of the world go by. It is an initiation into a kingdom, a fraternity of the saved. Thus, we must also worship God collectively and communally. "Wherever two or three are gathered," Jesus says, "I am there in the midst of them." The Christian assembly of prayer is the eucharistic sacrifice that Jesus inaugurated at the Last Supper. "Do this in commemoration of Me." The Mass is two things: it is first, a hearing of the Word of God, from the sacred texts and from the preacher, the minister of the word; secondly, it is the sacrifice of the Eucharist, in which bread and wine are changed into the body and blood of Jesus. The Eucharist is a true sacrifice as we offer the crucified Lord to the Father—"announcing the death of the Lord until He comes." And this sacrifice places at our disposal the prayer of incomparable value: it presents us the opportunity of giving something precious and completely satisfying to the Father, Christ His Son. Every true love demands giving, donation, an offering to the loved one. But what could we possibly ever offer God that would really be valuable to Him? Jesus gives us something—Himself, the Son of God, whom we can offer to the Father. This gift is so pleasing to God that He reciprocates by offering us his most precious gift—Jesus, who comes to us in communion, uniting Himself with us, serving as our food and strength.

Grace. Grace is a scriptural word that the preacher is handling frequently, and he should make sure that it conveys some meaning for his listeners. Grace is often either explained in a simplist moral fashion (it is something you get in baptism, lose by sin, and regain by penance) or in technical scholastic manner (grace is a created quality inhering in the substance of the soul, etc.). Neither explanation is really satisfactory for a contemporary congregation. The root meaning of the word grace in scripture (*charis,* as used so frequently by St. Paul) might provide better popular insight. Etymologically, the word grace means "favor"—in the sense of brooding over, or bending over, as a mother bends over her child with love, protection, kindness. When God gives us grace, He favors us, He bends over us with love, protection, kindness; and this favor takes the precise form of a real gift that changes us as persons—we are "favored," changed in the innermost depths of our being, drawn into the intimate life of God, protected by Him as His own sons.

Sacraments. Jesus promised us the continuing protection of the Holy Spirit who sustains us in our new life with God. It is particularly in the sacraments instituted by Jesus that this life is protected and developed. The preacher should explain Jesus' use of symbols and signs in the sacraments. The various symbols of the sacraments (the pouring of water, the eating of bread, the anointings) are the vehicles of God's grace, the rites during which God confers His grace. But the symbol also indicates the particular kind of grace that is being conferred: The pouring of water, a recollection of the washing process, shows us that in baptism a spiritual washing is taking place in which man is cleansed from the results of Adam's fall and restored to divine intimacy; the eating of bread, a recollection of the feeding process, shows us that in the Eucharist we are being fed by Jesus who is our life and the source of our strength; the anointing, which is a soothing and consoling and restorative human operation, shows us that in Anointing of the Sick, for example, the person is being calmed and consoled and prepared for his last journey.

The seven sacraments constitute God's life-long, protective, continuing intimacy with His sons. In baptism, we are reborn to God. In penance, we are restored to that life if we lose it by infidelity to God. Confirmation is the sacrament of Christian maturity in which God gives us added grace to live as an adult Christian in the world, to be a witness to Him, to endure everything for Him. The Eucharist is the sacrament of union and life: Jesus increases our union with Him and gives Himself to us as our food, the continuing sustenance we need to live as Christians. Matrimony and Holy Orders are the social sacraments: In matrimony, God gives the two partners the grace for a successful marriage with all the implications that entails; in holy orders, God selects a few members of the Christian community and gives them grace to serve as His ministers, interceding for the people of God, bringing the sacraments, preaching the word, serving them. In Anointing of the Sick, God bestows the graces necessary to maintain Christian perspective in the debilitating and bewildering moments of serious illness; and He prepares the individual for the final journey to God.

In addition to sanctifying grace conferred by the sacraments, God also gives us His instant protection at any moment that we need it. This is called actual grace: the protection and help of God, inspiring us in our minds to know what He wants us to do, and strengthening us in our hearts to do it. This is one more proof of God's infinite love for us and interest in us.

Joy in the Lord. At the Last Supper, Jesus stated, "These things I have spoken to you that My joy may be in you, and that your joy may be made full." The Christian life is essentially a joyful one: Jesus' message is *good* news. There are over five hundred precise commands in the scriptures to rejoice in the Lord: beginning with the Old Testament commands, "Serve the Lord in joy," "Rejoice all you just ones," "Children of Sion, rejoice and be glad in the Lord your God," and culminating in St. Paul's ringing cry, "Rejoice in the Lord always, again I say rejoice!" The Christian is joyful, despite the severe sufferings of life, because he is experiencing the love of Jesus; and the fruit of love is always joy. The Christian has the love of the Lord, a design for His life, the beginnings of resurrection within Him. He has every reason for being the most lighthearted of men. St. Paul writes: "Jesus is my joy; Jesus is my life."

Mary. Another figure looms large in the life of Jesus: the Virgin of Nazareth, the mother of the God-man. She appears in the opening scenes of the Gospel, receiving the angel Gabriel; she carries the Lord in her womb to visit her cousin Elizabeth; she gives birth to the Lord; she is intimately associated with His youth—in Bethlehem, in Nazareth, in Egypt, in Jerusalem; she offers Him to the Father in the temple; we see her at the fringes of the crowd during Jesus' preaching ministry; she stands beneath the cross when He is crucified; and finally we see her joined with the apostles in the upper room in the days before Pentecost. Christians from the earliest days of the Church recognized her unique place in Jesus' redeeming mission, and in a true spirit of Christian community they invoked her assistance from the kingdom of heaven. But they recognized her as more than merely one of the extremely favored elect; they recognized her as the Mother of all the redeemed. She freely accepted the Christ into the world (Christ who said: "I am the life"), and thus gave life to the world: She is the Mother of all those who have the life of Christ within them. And she continued her maternal role for souls—by offering Jesus to the Father in the temple, by joining Him at the foot of the cross on Golgotha, and by her constant interest and love for us in heaven. "Behold your mother," Jesus said of her from the cross. Christians have always respected her, imitated her, turned to her as their mother, sought a closer union with Jesus through her maternal assistance. She said: "All generations will call me blessed." This statement from *The Constitution on the Church* approved by Vatican Council II should serve as a guide to the preacher when he discusses the Virgin Mary:

> This most Holy Synod . . . exhorts theologians and preachers of the divine word to abstain zealously both from all gross exaggerations as well as from petty narrow-mindedness in considering the singular dignity of the Mother of God . . . Let them assiduously keep away from whatever, either by word or deed, could lead separated brethren or any other into error regarding the true doctrine of the Church. Let the faithful remember moreover that true devotion consists neither in sterile or transitory affection, nor in a certain vain credulity, but proceeds from true faith, by which we are led to know the excellence of the Mother of God, and we are moved to a filial love toward our Mother and to the imitation of her virtues.

3. MORAL.

A doctor of the law asked Jesus to tell him which was the greatest commandment of the law, and the Lord replied: "You shall love the Lord your God with your whole heart, and with your whole soul, and with your whole mind. This is the greatest and the first commandment. And the second is like it: You shall love your neighbor as yourself. On these two commandments depend the whole law and the prophets."

In the mind of Jesus, therefore, our obligation is to love. And this is what St. Paul said: "Love, therefore, is the fulfillment of the law." The ten commandments are an extension and articulation of our obligation to love God and our fellow men, and the preacher should present them that way. The first commandment concerns our obligation to love God, the second requires us to reverence Him, and the third to worship Him. The fourth commands filial love. The fifth requires us to love our neighbor by not hurting him. The sixth and ninth are concerned with the reverence and respect due to the bodies of our neighbors and the respect due to another's marriage. The seventh and tenth require us to respect our neighbor's property. The eighth commands us to be considerate of our neighbor by being honest and truthful with him. Love for God and love for our fellow man—that is our obligation.

Jesus adds a refinement to the law of love for our neighbors by asking us to love them as He loves us—by seeing our neighbors' true spiritual worth as a son of God, by forgiving them, by suffering for them if necessary. Thus Jesus summarizes it: "If you love Me, keep My commandments." This is the necessary demand of our union with him.

Control. When the original forebears of the human race, Adam and Eve, deserted God by their infidelity, they made us heirs to their ensuing condition—an unfortunate and annoying inclination to evil. Thus our initial reactions to people are not always noble and loving. Instead of loving people, we often tend to dominate and use them. Instead of respecting our neighbor, we often defile and despoil him. Our love, in other words, is not always automatic; it must be sustained and directed by discipline. The incisive Biblical word used to describe this process is "mortification," literally a killing or destroying. St. Paul, accordingly, writes to the Colossians, "Mortify your members," and what he means is that we must kill and destroy any of our reactions that would violate love: self-interest, self-gratification, disrespect for others. And this must be an uncompromising procedure—that is the significance of Jesus' metaphorical statement that if one's eye is an occasion of sin, one should pluck it out, or if one's hand is an occasion of sin, it should be amputated. Love is the supreme value and we should destroy any reaction of ours that might debase it. This requires discipline and control, but the Lord will give us the strength necessary to sustain love if we remain close to Him. ("My grace is sufficient for you.")

Sex. Throughout the entire Old Testament there was evident a healthy, balanced view of sexual morality. Sex was good and holy, and only an abuse of it was wrong. The Song of Songs is lyrical about the value and inherent beauty of sex—in fact, it is used as the figure of the soul's union with God. Jesus did nothing to abrogate that mentality; he only delineated more carefully some aspects of the sanctity of marriage: divorce and adultery of the heart. But later philosophies began to see something inherently wrong and perverse in sex itself: Manichaeism, Jansenism, Puritanism, among others. The preacher must be careful that these un-Christian philosophies do not infiltrate his preaching and lead him to present sex as something slightly tainted. Sex is good—so good and holy and beautiful and romantic that God wants His children to share it with only one person.

In presenting the moral law and sin to his listeners, the preacher might keep in mind the words of Pope John XXIII to the Lenten preachers in 1960:

> Beloved sons! Do not give too much thought to stressing the negative aspects of life . . . Harsh words, pessimism, and barbed arguments are out of place on a priest's lips. Nor is it necessary for him to go into the detailed descriptions of evil upon which the morbid imagination of the weak likes to linger. Just a hint, one word rather than two, must suffice.

Pardon. "But if anyone sins," writes St. John, "we have an advocate with the Father, Jesus Christ the just, and He is a propitiation for our sins, not for ours only but also for those of the whole world." Thus the preacher's discussion of sin must be followed by a discussion of God's mercy. Jesus is the good shepherd who forgives and forgives—even as He forgave His executioners at the last moment on the cross: "Father forgive them for they know not what they do." Whenever we return to Jesus, promising to leave Him no more, He receives us without reproach or recrimination. Perhaps the most moving dialogue in all scripture is that between Jesus and Peter after the resurrection when the Lord meets the disciple who had denied Him. There are no harsh words on the Lord's lips; only his probing, pleading question repeated three times to Peter: "Do you love Me?"

The sins of others. Jesus is quite insistent, however, that we be not censorious about others' sins. "Do not judge," He says, "that you may not be judged. Why do you see the speck in your brother's eye, and do not see the beam in your own eye?" And when He forgave the woman apprehended in adultery, He said sternly to her accusers: "Let whoever is without sin cast the first stone." Spiritual arrogance or hauteur is a danger that the Christian soul must avoid. Jesus was stern and severe only toward the scribes and Pharisees, those people who made a pretense of religion by following a precise program of rite and ritual and then condemning the sins and faults of others. "Hypocrites! Whitened sepulchers!"

Freedom. Jesus said: "If you abide in my word, you shall be my disciples indeed, and you shall know the truth, and the truth shall make you free." His listeners asked Him what He meant by this freedom, and He answered: "I say to you, everyone who commits sin is a slave to sin." This is a fundamental concept of the good news, an idea that St. Paul develops in his epistles: that sin is a servitude, and fidelity to God sets us free. The man who is caught in his sins is tied and bound to his compulsions and desires; his vision is narrowed to his own nagging interests; he is a slave to his whims. But the man who is faithful to God is freed from all that: He has the love of Jesus; the world is his; the seeds of resurrection are within him. He is a free man. He is a happy man.

4. SOCIAL.

Jesus incorporates us in His kingdom, a community of those who have been redeemed and belong to the Lord. This is the church the Lord founded. When the preacher discusses the church he should not be so impressed by the organizational and institutional aspects of the church that he neglects the spiritual inner dynamism of this new kingdom. Certainly, the Lord chose a number of the original disciples to be His leaders, and He vested them with His authority: "He who hears you, hears Me" and "You will sit upon twelve thrones judging the twelve tribes of Israel." And he established one of these original disciples as primate, giving him the power of the keys and the authority to bind and loosen. (Our English name *Peter* does not convey the impact of the new Aramaic name *Kepha*, rock, which Jesus gave to the head of the apostles. *Kepha* was translated into its Greek counterpart *Petros* from the word for rock, *petra*.) That was the organization of the functioning church we observe in the Acts of the Apostles, the church to which Jesus promised "I am with you all days, even unto the end of time," the church against which the gates of hell would never prevail.

But the church is more than an efficient organization for accomplishing religious objectives: It is the family of God, the continuing body of Christ. In the Old Testament, God established a covenant (agreement) with His chosen people, and as revelation progressed He promised a new covenant, a new chosen people: He said to His people through Jeremiah, "I will make a new covenant with the house of Israel and the house of Judah; I will give my law in their hearts, and I will write it in their hearts, and I will be their God, and they shall be My people." The early Christian understood the church in this sense of covenant, the new people of God. One of St. Paul's favorite expressions for the members of the church was "God's holy people" (which has been inadequately translated in the past as "saints"), and "holy" in this context does not necessarily imply moral rectitude, but sacred or chosen or protected. Through Christ, we are grouped in one family, one body—the body of Christ. He is our head, our leader, and together with Him we will all work for the growth and extension of His family.

Christian Engagement. However, the family of God is not to be a separatist movement. We are called to love all men, not with a cold, institutionalized charity, but with a warm, Christlike love. "Love is the fulfillment of the Law." In response to the question, "Who is my neighbor," Jesus told the parable of the good Samaritan, indicating that any human being is my neighbor, even this unknown beaten chap lying in the road and needing my help. The Lord wants us to love everybody, even those who are not particularly agreeable to us. He said: "For if you love those who love you, what reward shall you have? Do not even the publicans do that?" And love here implies recognition of value in the other person, acceptance of him as he realistically is, reverence for his person. Preachers sometimes limit the vast depths of Christian love to a negative endurance of annoying people. But Jesus wants our love to be positive, reaching out to every man. In describing the final judgment, Jesus indicates the necessity of this positive love. "Come, blessed ones, take possession of the kingdom prepared for you from the beginning of the world, for I was hungry and you gave Me something to eat; I was thirsty, and you gave Me something to drink; I was a stranger, and you gave Me shelter; naked and you covered Me; sick and you visited Me; I was in prison and you came to Me." When did we do these things for *You,* they ask. And Jesus responds: "As long as you did it for one of these, the least of My brothers, you did it for Me." This, then, is the dimension of our love: we are to see Jesus Himself in every human being. The Christian must have a highly developed social conscience: There should be no work, no charity, no need, no necessity, no emergency foreign to His love. "I am all things to all men," St. Paul said.

Forgiveness. This love also includes forgiveness of injury, as Jesus forgave His executioners from the cross. "If you are offering your gift at the altar," the Lord said, "and you remember that your brother has something against you, leave your gift before the altar and go first to be reconciled to your brother, and then come and offer your gift." And Peter asked how many times we should forgive people. Seven times? "No," the Lord said, "seventy times seven times." This is an infinite number, of course, and means that we must forgive and forgive—as Christ forgives us. "Forgive us our trespasses, as we forgive those who trespass against us"—that is the perspective Jesus asks us to keep in mind.

Apostolate. The Christian is to be engaged, involved with every human being, working, serving, assisting, helping. "I did not come to be served, but to serve," Jesus said, and He left us a remarkable demonstration of that when He washed the disciples' feet at the Last Supper. The church is, as Isiah prophesies, a servant church, ministering to the needs of all people. Of all human needs, the greatest is spiritual; and every Christian—priest and layman—is called to bring the message and comfort of Jesus to men. We are all called to be apostles—by witness, by proclamation, by service, by instruction. "You are to be witnesses to Me in Jerusalem, in Samaria, and even to the ends of the earth."

When the original disciples were engaged in their early ministry they were working miracles in Jesus' name; but they encountered one case of a boy seized by an unclean spirit where they seemed helpless to do anything. They asked the Lord why they were unable to cure him. "This kind is cast out only by prayer and fasting," Jesus answered, underscoring the apostolic need for prayer and penance. We must work for our brothers—and we must pray for them, make sacrifices, too. People need the light, they need *charis,* and *charis* is obtained for them by asking the Lord.

The World. The Christian is to be engaged in his own society, and as the preacher explains the Christian's role in the world, he should be careful that he does not descend into a hellenistic dualism, describing the spirit as good and matter as evil. Gnostic theories have always camped at the edges of authentic religion, but these have no relation to the good news. In the account of creation in the first book of scripture, there is a recurring phrase when God creates each area of matter: "And God saw that it was good." And when the totality is created: "And God saw all the things that He had made, and they were very good." Creation is good, and God's world is good. Whenever scripture condemns the world, it is not condemning God's good world of matter, but the spirit of sin in the world, the sin of those who would divorce this world from God. The Son of God took our flesh, and He will resurrect our whole being, *flesh* and spirit. Christianity is not a spiritualistic mode of life where we live in higher regions of the spirit and despise this material world in which we live. We are to use and enjoy and value God's good world. That is why in establishing the sacramental system, Jesus used bread and oil and salt and wine and water—these good material things. The Christian life is a human, joyful, grateful existence, full of wonder for the richness and beauty of God's creation and His people. We are to live in the kingdom of God, which begins here in this world and is completed in the new Jerusalem—and God's kingdom is good. Pope Paul VI in an address in St. Peter's Basilica on Christmas Day, 1964, echoes this spirit of the true Christian attuned to life:

> It is necessary to awaken in the paper, iron and cement heart of modern man the urge for human sympathy, for simple, pure and generous love, for poetry, for natural and living things.

5. ESCHATALOGICAL.

St. John reminds us: "God is love." The program of our life should be to return that love, to respond to God, to choose Him freely. Love necessarily entails a choice: If we truly love someone, we choose him or her in preference to someone else. That is the reason that in the Old Testament sin is so frequently called "adultery" or "fornication"—because it implies a turning away from God, a choice of something else, and the most graphic and meaningful image the Jewish writers could conceive was physical infidelity where the wrong person was chosen, where there was unfaithfulness to the one who should be loved. If we love God and choose Him, then we will possess Him forever; but if we reject Him and sin against Him, we automatically choose something else, and we have lost God. This constitutes the platform of Jesus' eschatalogical message: At the end of life, there will be a judgment of whether or not we have chosen God.

Death. Christ's message about death is simple and forthright: preparedness. Death is the termination point of one phase of our existence, the painful moment that must be endured by all descendents of Adam. Jesus wants us to be prepared to meet it. He tells the parable of the wise and foolish virgins, the ones who were ready to meet the bridegroom and the ones who missed Him because they were unprepared. And He speaks of the vigilant servant: "Blessed are those servants whom the master shall find watching on his return." He reminds us that death can come like a thief in the night, at an unknown and unexpected hour. And he summarizes His teaching: "What I say to you, I say to all—watch!" Of course, death for the Christian is not the final dissolution of existence; it is the beginning of life with the risen Jesus. St. Paul writes: "Our Savior Jesus Christ has destroyed death and brought to light life and incorruption by the good news of which I have been appointed a preacher."

Hell. Pope John XXIII said to the Lenten preachers in 1959: "God has called upon us to heal our brothers, not to frighten them." This is particularly applicable when the preacher discusses the fact of hell. Such a discussion is no time for pyrotechnics or hysterical oratory—we are discussing the saddest fact in life: the loss of God. If, through the pattern of his life, a person has rejected God's love and mercy, if he chooses something else and refuses to be reconciled with God, he has condemned himself to the loss of Jesus—and that is what hell is. We only have one lifetime to use, and in the framework of those years we must choose Jesus; but if we fail to respond, if we do not listen to the good news, if we do not seek the limitless mercy of Jesus ("seventy times seven times"), then we have made our decision. And when the full impact of that decision weighs upon the lost soul, he is in utter agony, for there is no torment in the world equal to the loss of love—"what might have been." The agony of loss is the fundamental suffering of hell, but the body also participates in this great calamity. The body rises with the soul in resurrection, and it also falls with the soul in damnation and is subjected to the fires of hell. (Again, the fundamental union between body and soul in Christian teaching.) But does this agony have to last forever? Yes, because if you cherish and develop love, it goes on and on; but if you kill it, it is dead forever. Such is the nature of love.

The Paschal Mystery. Christian preachers have not always done justice to the resurrection of Jesus: They have often limited their discussion to a consideration of an historical fact or an apologetic argument. But the resurrection is more than that. It is the fact of our resurrection with Jesus—not at some future time, but now at this very moment in which we live. Jesus is, as St. Paul calls Him, the firstborn from the dead. He rises from the dead and draws us with Him. We who live with Jesus (*in* Jesus, to use St. Paul's frequent phrase) share in His resurrection, and we have the seeds of resurrection in us as the result of our baptism—the process is under way. The early Christians were vitally aware of this situation, and St. Paul writes to the Ephesians almost as if the process were already completed:

> But God, who is rich in mercy, by reason of his very great love with which he has loved us even when we were dead by reason of our sins, brought us to life together with Christ (by grace you have been saved), and raised us up together, and seated us together in heaven in Christ Jesus.

In the resurrection Jesus will finally bring us to heaven, the new Jerusalem where, in St. John's words, "They shall hunger no more, nor thirst, neither shall the sun fall on them nor any heat. God will wipe away all tears from their eyes, and there shall be no more death, nor mourning, nor crying, nor sorrow, for the former things have passed away." Our bodies will be glorified ("this corruptible body will put on incorruptibility") just as Jesus Himself was glorified during those days on earth after the resurrection. We will experience the loving companionship of our brothers, our friends in the kingdom of God. But most of all, we will receive the full impact of loving God, our joy and our happiness and our ecstasy. St. Paul: "We see now through a mirror in an obscure manner, but then face to face." And: "Eye has not seen nor ear heard, nor has it entered into the heart of man what things God has prepared for those who love Him."

This moment of the resurrection is the historical moment in which we should live, the Christian moment. The early Christian never worshiped Jesus as ascended and gone, but rather Jesus as alive, resurrected, here. Their prayers always concluded with a petition to Jesus "who *lives* and *reigns* forever." We are children of the resurrection, living that moment constantly and continually. That is the secret of the Christian's gigantic joy. Jesus lives, and we have the seeds of resurrection within us; we can lose them by infidelity to

God (but why would we want to do that?); we are members of the kingdom of God, living in joy and peace with our brothers, here now in this phase of the kingdom, and soon forever in the new Jerusalem. The resurrection is truly the *good* news.

The above paragraphs indicate some of the basic themes of the good news, the message that the Christian preacher should communicate to his listeners. He must take these themes and relate them to his contemporary audience, choosing the proper language, providing compelling illustrations, engaging the interest of his listeners. The good news is as good today as it was two thousand years ago, but the preacher must tell it to his modern listeners so they can understand and value it.

The preacher must preach the entire good news, not just a part of it that might perhaps appeal to him. Jesus presents us with a total way of life, and the preacher must communicate that total picture. When he does not, problems ensue. If a preacher only preaches the eschatalogical doctrine without the social doctrine, he can fall into illuminism. The moral doctrine without the religious and eschatalogical produces moralisms. The social without the religious results in natural social work. And the religious without the social degenerates into pietisms. The preacher's mission is to preach Jesus' message—all of it.

Then he will be a true herald of the good news.

EXERCISES

Remember the definition of a Christian preacher: One who preaches the good news enthusiastically.

Ask yourself some searching questions:

· Am I preaching the good news of Jesus Christ? Or:

· Is my teaching mainly derivative, taken from later Christian authors, with only a passing reference to the original *kerygma*?

· Have I been preaching an illuminism—pie in the sky, and let the rest of the world go by?

· Has Jansenism made inroads in my preaching—a dualism between matter and spirit in which matter is corrupt and human activities tainted?

· Have I been influenced by Pelagianism—spiritual living is basically a rigid perfectionism, all ethic and little love?

· Have I been preaching only moralisms—a dour, accusatory

form of preaching that separates the moral content from the rest of the good news?

· Have I been guilty of hysterical eschatology—pyrotechnics about hell's fires rather than a sober discussion about life's greatest calamity: the loss of God.

· Is my preaching sentimental—hearts and flowers and holy cards rather than the real and dynamic love of Jesus?

· Remember: the good news of Jesus can be summarized under five headings:

1. Incarnational.
2. Religious.
3. Moral.
4. Social.
5. Eschatalogical.

· Review the good news as it is outlined in this chapter.

· Do not forget: the good news must be preached with all the dynamics of effective public speaking—the speaker's mentality, the ASRM principle, the conversational mode.

· Review these principles from Part I.

SCRIPTURE

A true incident: One of America's most distinguished preachers was standing in a sacristy one day after delivering a sermon, and he found himself being congratulated by a gentleman from the congregation. The preacher later recounted the dialogue. The gentleman, well-dressed and intelligent, was expressing admiration for the sermon.

"It was an excellent sermon, Father."

"Thank you very much."

"But do you know, for the entire first half of your sermon I was unconvinced about what you were discussing."

"Oh."

"But when you started to quote Scripture, I became convinced. I said, you know this isn't just a priest expressing his own ideas. It's God himself speaking. Then I believed you."

This episode illustrates once again the undeniable persuasiveness that Scripture has for the average Christian in our audiences. There is something unique and entirely special about Scripture; and that, of course, derives from the altogether singular nature of the book—the inspired word of God. When the preacher quotes the Scriptures he speaks with the same impact as did the prophets of the Old Testament when they cried out, "The Lord God says!" Every time the Christian preacher relates something from Scripture or quotes the exact words of Jesus or explains the good news from the pages of the Bible, his remarks have that same dazzling effect on the audience—the Lord God says!

In the early church the use of Scripture occupied a privileged position. The new kingdom of God inherited the traditional Jewish

reverence for the inspired books, and the herald of the good news
continued the rabbi's function of explaining the law and the
prophets to his congregation. There were not, of course, many
manuscripts available, but the Scriptures were memorized, quoted,
and used extensively by the ministers of the gospel in their preaching. St. Paul's classic advice to Timothy reflects this Biblical orienta-
tion:

> For from your infancy you have known the Sacred
> Writings, which are able to instruct you unto salvation
> by the faith which is in Christ Jesus. All scripture is
> inspired by God and useful for teaching, for reproving,
> for correcting, for instructing in justice; that the man
> of God may be perfect, equipped for every good work.

Biblical preaching established itself as the Christian form of
preaching during the age of the apostles and during the Patristic
era. The homilies of the church Fathers were basically discussions
of Scripture as related to the contemporary audiences. This tradition endured until at least the late middle ages when subtle and
unhappy changes began to occur in Christian preaching. With the
ascendancy of high scholasticism, Scripture was used more and more
in an argumentative and apologetic vein to prove a thesis or conclusion already formulated—in distinction to the original tradition
of using Scripture in the objective sense as a receptacle of the good
news. This led the way to the introduction into the homiletic tradition of those errant philosophies we discussed in the preceding
chapter. Scripture was not preached, it was used for the speaker's
own purposes. The argument was first formulated, and then Scripture was added, as a cook adds garnish to an already-prepared
meal.

The net result was a lessening enthusiasm for utilizing Scripture
in preaching. Derivative sources were used more frequently, and
Scripture was often used indifferently and carelessly, almost as an
afterthought. Whole generations of preachers appeared who had no
acquaintance with the Old Testament, and whose only contact with
the New Testament was in the pages of the pious books they read.

The Christian renewal sponsored by Vatican II seeks to correct
these misdirections wherever they exist. The current homiletic
movement within the church is stressing a return to a biblically
oriented preaching, a greater use of Scripture in preaching the

word of God. If the Christian preacher is to be the *keryx*, the herald of the good news, he must know this good news, he must use it, he must preach it to the people.

The contemporary preacher again needs to submit himself to a searching examination: Is he using Scripture in his sermons—using it the way the original heralds of the good news used it? This does not imply that a sermon is to be a disquisition on Scripture, with a line-by-line analysis and exegesis. But it does mean that the preacher should draw the objective content of his sermon from the *kerygma*, the core of the apostolic teaching as it is found in the pages of Scripture—it means, in a word, that he should preach the good news. And it also means that he should use scriptural texts in his sermon, quoting the words of Jesus, explaining the Christian commitment as it is described in the Bible, illustrating his material with episodes from the biblical texts. The preacher should not pepper the text of his sermon with scriptural references and then machine gun them at his audience. He should, though, use Scripture prudently and judiciously and meaningfully, applying it to his modern listeners. He must preach a contemporary sermon, in contemporary idiom, with contemporary illustrations, with relevancy to his contemporary audience; but he must know his Scripture and use it intelligently and incisively in his sermon. Then his sermon will have that rare Christian flavor that only the inspired word of God can provide.

From the viewpoint of public speaking alone, the use of Scripture offers tremendous advantages to the preacher. The audience reacts to it and is engaged by it because it is 1) authoritative, 2) real, and 3) human.

1. *Authoritative.* Scripture is, as we have indicated, a clinching argument in the persuasive process. When the preacher throws the weight of Scripture behind his words, his listeners must say: "That's it—that's what God wants." What more could a public speaker ask for in attempting to practice the art of persuasion?

2. *Real.* The stories, incidents, and episodes from the New Testament are concerned with real historical characters. Most of the characters in pages of the Old Testament are real historical persons, although a few of them are allegorical figures used to dramatize a religious idea, such as Judith and Esther. But the recounting of real episodes by the public speaker has great impact on an audience, as we explained in our previous discussion of emotion in pub-

lic speaking: The real engages our emotions most effectively. As the preacher discusses these real persons from Scripture, the audience follows intently. This is fact, not fiction. Jesus and His disciples, Matthew and John and Peter and the others—these are real people. Judas and Pilate, the woman at the well in Samaria, the centurion— all true historical characters. When your listeners hear these episodes, they become engaged; because, as we indicated, people enjoy stories about other people. The Bible is a treasury of these real stories.

3. *Human.* Not only are the episodes in the pages of Scripture real, they are also human. The figures of the Bible are not presented as clinical and detached case histories; they are presented as flesh and blood people, full of human emotion, flowing with the juices of life. The audience becomes quickly involved with them and even begins to identify with them. We feel for them, we sympathize with them, we understand them—and in so doing, we understand ourselves better. Peter is a pathetic figure as he stands in the courtyard warming himself by the fire during Jesus' arrest. In the bewilderment of that strange moment he denies his master, and later he must re-establish his friendship with Jesus—"Simon, son of John, do you love me?" "Lord, you know all things, you know that I love you." This is the stuff of human drama. Or Pilate, the practical politician, caught in the dilemma between his conscience and his political future. David, the shining champion of the Lord, becoming entangled in his infatuation for Urias' wife Bethsabee, and driving himself to the crimes his passion urges. Josue, exasperated with his followers, trying to goad them on to the conquest of Jericho. The Canaanite woman pleading with Jesus to cure her sick daughter, refusing to be hushed by the disciples until the Lord helped her. This is strong material, guaranteed to involve your audience.

Homiletic material that is authoritative, real, and human: that is what the Bible offers. If the preacher uses the Scripture wisely he has in his hand a tool of incalculable value. It is, therefore, crucially important that he master this tool and learn how to use it wisely. This process can be accomplished in two ways:

1. READ AND PONDER THE TEXT.

There is only one known human method for mastering a book, whether it be the *Iliad, Das Kapital,* or the Bible: Read it carefully, and ponder it! In this digest age, with its capsulated programs and its condensed versions, there is a disaffection for the precise business of earnest study and careful reflection. But there is no substitute for it, either. If you want to master a book, you must read it and reread it, ponder it, reflect upon it until the book is yours, until you know the contents and are able to use them, quote them, and relate them. This is what the herald of Christ must do with the Scriptures. He must master this book, make it his own. He must read it and reread it; he must ponder it and reflect upon it. This is his task—and it is a lifetime one.

The preacher is obliged to present Jesus to his listeners, but not in a clinical manner as a doctor might present a case history, nor in a reportorial fashion as a news commentator might report a news event, nor even in a dramatic manner as an actor might re-create an historical figure. The preacher's presentation of Jesus to the audience is more subtle and difficult than any of those presentations— he must present Jesus in the manner of a personal introduction, a real person-to-person encounter between the living, risen Lord and the people in this audience today. The essence of religion is experience with the Lord, and Christ invites us to companionship: "I call you now not servants, but friends." When we say that we must know Jesus, we are not speaking of a speculative, theoretical knowledge, but a personal, immediate knowledge, the kind that joins us to our friends and loved ones. This is the kind of personal knowledge Jesus speaks of when He says: "I am the good shepherd, and I know mine and mine know me." And the kind of knowledge St. Paul speaks of in Philippians when he states he wants to gain Christ:

> . . . so that I may know him and the power of his resurrection and the fellowship of his suffering: become like to him in death, in the hope that somehow I may attain to the resurrection from the dead.

To present Jesus to the audience in the manner of a personal introduction demands that the preacher himself know Jesus. He must contact Him in prayer, but he must also study Him in the Scriptures, learn what He said and did, how He thought about things, what kind of person He was. This requires careful reading and reflection, but it is worth it, for then the preacher can present the person of Jesus to his listeners. But if he is unable to do this, the Lord can say to him those same sad words He said to the Pharisees: "You know neither me nor My father."

Reflection on the Scriptures furthermore affords the preacher a greater insight into the message of Jesus. A hurried, careless reading of the Bible can only give one a surface understanding of what the Lord is really saying. But a precise reading of the texts and thoughtful reflection about them can open up whole new vistas of understanding for the preacher and his audiences. For example, the well-known parable of the sower and the seed, which is used as the gospel for Sexagesima Sunday, recounts the story of a farmer who sowed some seed on a footpath, on rocky ground, among thorns, and on good soil; then the Lord explains the parable as the word of God being received in various ways. A cursory explanation by a preacher might consist in a statement that we have to receive the word of God and not choke it out. But there is much more to the parable than that. The Lord says: "The seed is the word of God." ("The word of God" is a frequent phrase in Scripture, representing the dynamic, grace-giving message of the good news—a concept we will discuss in the following chapter.) "And those on the footpath are those who hear, but the devil comes and takes the word out of their hearts lest they should believe and be saved." Those on the rocky ground receive the word with joy, but they have no roots and thus believe for a time and then fall away in time of temptation. The seed in the thorns are those who hear and make progress but become stifled by the cares and riches and pleasures of life, and ultimately do not mature. But the seed on good ground are those who hear the word, retain it, and bear fruit. The pivotal concept is that grace is a growing, dynamic thing that must mature; the "state of grace" is not merely a static thing that you either have or do not have. You either grow in the life of Christ (in line with St. Paul's statement: "Grow up in all things in him who is the head, Christ.") or you will deteriorate. Then Jesus describes the four possible reactions to the grace of Jesus Christ: 1) those who listen to the invitation of Jesus but it has no impact on them and they disregard it (the footpath); 2) those who become enthusiastically religious, but their reaction is shallow and they abandon Jesus in temptation when things get difficult (rocky ground); 3) those who become genuinely religious but stunt their growth because of involvement in cares and riches and pleasure (thorns); 4) those who become fully developed in the love of Jesus (the good ground). The Lord presents us a definitive schema of the varieties of Christian experience, a precise outline of the possibilities of our relationship with God. Later Christian writers have often been intrigued with inventing different categories of religious perfection: ladders and mountains and scales to indicate our exact position with God. But what could be more clear or more satisfying than this schema by Jesus himself? The preacher can use this parable and ask his listeners: What kind of Christian are you? What category do you fit into? You belong in one of these four categories, because Jesus has covered all contingencies. Do you disregard the invitation of Jesus (footpath)? Are you exteriorly religious, with lots of noise and hand-clapping, but interiorly so shallow that you desert Jesus when any interesting temptation appears (rocky ground)? Are you a serious lover of the Lord, but retarded from a closer relationship because of your involvement in your own cares and self-interests (thorns)? Or do you really love God, receiving his grace "with nobility and goodness of heart," doing what he wants, becoming involved in him (good ground)? Answer the question for yourself. Examine the four categories. What kind of Christian are you?

Reflection on the Scripture, then, can unveil these new horizons in the message of Jesus. But you will not increase your understanding of Scripture and gain greater insights if you flip through it like an illustrated magazine. You need to read carefully and then ponder.

Scripture provides us not only with the message of Jesus, but also with the example of Jesus. "Jesus began to do and teach," St. Luke tells us, indicating that the Lord was the perfect illustration of those things he preached. Accordingly, the preacher can, if he knows his Scripture, present Jesus as the engaging illustration of the Christian doctrine. Practically all of the things the preacher will be discussing can be supported by incidents from the life of Jesus. Forgiveness: Jesus hanging on the cross praying the Father to forgive his executioners because they know not what they do. Prayer: Jesus frequently slipping away from the Apostles to pray or rising early in the morning to be discovered praying on the mountainside; or Jesus gathered with the apostles in the eucharistic service of the Last Supper. Equilibrium during suffering: Jesus in agony of spirit while praying in the garden of Gethsemane the night before his death—"O, my father, if it is possible, let this chalice pass me by; but, let your will be done, not mine." These powerful illustrations are in the pages of Scripture, for the man who knows the book.

The person of Jesus. The message of Jesus. The example of Jesus.

These are what the preacher can have at his disposal—if he reads the Scripture carefully, and ponders it.

2. CONSULT BACKGROUND SOURCES.

Scripture is the preacher's tool, and the more he knows about this tool the more effectively he can use it. Thus, some background reading in Scripture would be extremely valuable. The kind of background reading that would prove helpful to the average preacher is not necessarily the technical, professional material that appears to the Scripture scholar: for example, technical discussions of the root meaning of some Aramaic verb, or the use of the word *oikonomos* in the New Testament. The average preacher, however, should be able to gather valuable material from serious and intelligent works about Scripture that are directed to a general reader: for example, the various established lives of Christ, those by Lagrange and Pratt, or the more popular works by Goodier and Daniel-Rops; and the refreshing abundance of scriptural books and articles being published today about the figures of the Old Testament, the prophets, salvation history, the New Testament personalities, the parables of our Lord, the doctrine of the Epistles. These works help the preacher to understand the Scriptures better and thus communicate the good news more effectively to his listeners.

Background reading in Scripture provides three precise services for the preacher: It helps him to enhance the sense of realism about Scripture; it helps him to understand the exact meaning of the text; and it presents him with the scriptural insights other men of God might have into the Scriptures.

1. The episodes related in the Bible happened at a precise historical moment, in a specific geographical and cultural situation. The more the preacher knows about the history and geography and culture of the epoch in which the episode is set, the more realistic he will be able to make it for his listeners. And anything that can enhance the sense of realism will necessarily increase audience involvement. If, for example, you understand the political climate of Palestine during the lifetime of Jesus, you will be able to make many of the episodes in the Gospel much more realistic. Palestine during Christ's life was an occupied country, much in the manner of nations that are today occupied by military forces; this explains Pilate's position in Jerusalem as the regent of the occupying forces, and it explains his dilemma at the trial of Jesus when he was caught

between his allegiance to his superiors in Rome and these Jewish natives of the conquered country. Another example: The Samaritans were the despised outcasts, the religious heretics in the north, and an understanding of this situation gives added impact to Jesus' story about the good Samaritan. Know the background, and you will increase the sense of realism.

2. Such reading can also increase our comprehension of the precise meaning of the text. In the sermon on the mount, for instance, Jesus says: "And whoever forces you to go for one mile, go two miles with him." What does that mean? There was a provision in the Roman law for occupied countries that if a Roman soldier were carrying baggage or any other object he could force any native he might encounter to carry his load for the space of one mile. And one can only imagine with what anger a Jew carried a Roman soldier's load, and with what vehemence he dropped it to the ground at the exact end of one mile. In context, Jesus is discussing love for our fellow men, and he tells his Jewish audience that if they are forced to carry a soldier's load they should carry it *two miles* instead of the prescribed one mile! He is, therefore, calling for heroism in love: love that knows no bounds, love that serves and endures even under such tyranny and oppression as this. But you only get the full dimension of the Lord's words if you know the background. Or, in the parable of the prodigal son, Jesus is describing the fallen condition of the boy and he says, "And he went and joined one of the citizens of that country, who sent him to his farm to feed swine. And he longed to fill his stomach with the pods the swine were eating, but no one offered to give any to him." If you know the cultural and religious feeling of the Jews about swine, you will understand Christ's full intent in the parable. Here is this boy yearning to eat the food fed to the swine, and he has fallen so low that he cannot even obtain it. The Jews regarded swine as dirty and defiled; they could not eat it, and they were not even allowed to touch the animals themselves. And yet this boy is feeding them, desiring their food—he has fallen to the lowest possible state of degradation in the Jewish mind. Jesus' point is this: no matter how low you have fallen, no matter how heinous your crimes, the merciful Father is still waiting on the hill for you—waiting to fall upon you, kill the fatted calf, make merry. The background supplies this added insight into the Lord's words.

3. Collateral reading can furthermore give you the insights other

thinkers have gathered from the scriptural texts. The study of Scripture is an endless, lifelong task: The more we read and ponder, the more we see and understand. This personal comprehension has been shared by many students of the Bible in the pages of their books and articles. Daniel-Rops, for example, in discussing Jesus' resurrection relates the episode of Mary Magdalen's first apparition of the Lord near the tomb. She is alone, weeping, confused. The Lord appears, but in her turmoil she does not recognize him; she thinks it is the gardener. A short dialogue ensues. Jesus asks her why she is weeping and whom she is seeking, and Mary inquires where they have taken the body. Then abruptly Jesus injects one word: "Mary!" In the pronunciation of her own name Mary immediately recognizes Jesus. Daniel-Rops' point is that the loved one can pronounce your name in inflections that are more meaningful than anyone else's use of your name. He writes:

> "This one word sufficed to reawaken in Magdalen the ardor and certainty of her faith. What Christian has not dreamed of hearing it, the word with which, from all eternity, God calls each one of us, but which the deaf do not hear."

Daniel-Rops offers an intriguing insight for the preacher: At the moment of our resurrection, Jesus will pronounce our name as we have never heard it pronounced before, with all the accents and inflections of one who loves us more than anyone else in the world. "What Christian has not dreamed of hearing it . . ." This is the kind of scriptural reflection that Christian thinkers can share with us and that we in turn can pass on to our listeners.

Reading Scripture, pondering it, consulting collateral authors— these are the ways to master the Bible. And the preacher should want to master it, because it contains the good news. And he is the herald of the good news.

EXERCISES

• A question for the preacher: Are you using Scripture in your sermons—using it the way the original heralds of the good news used it?

   • As a source of the good news?

   • As a reference of texts and quotations and illustrations?

• Recall the advantages of a judicious use of Scripture in the preacher's role as public speaker:

• Scripture is authoritative: "The Lord God says . . ."

• Scripture is real: It is concerned with real, historical persons who engage the interest of your listeners.

• Scripture is human: The people of Scripture are flesh and blood people, fully developed characters who evoke sympathy and identification from your listeners.

Learn how to use the invaluable tool of Scripture:

1. By reading and pondering the text so that you can present the person of Jesus, the message of Jesus, and the example of Jesus.

2. By consulting background sources so that you can increase the sense of realism in your scriptural presentation; understand the full meaning of the texts (remember the "second mile"); and share the insights of other friends of the Lord.

3

THE HOMILY

Scene: A priest preaching in a pulpit. Time: Sunday morning. Place: Anywhere, U.S.A. Conditions: Difficult.

The priest in the pulpit on a Sunday morning is working under conditions that are far from ideal for the public speaker. In fact, the situation is one that any experienced and professional public speaker might find discouraging. First of all, the preacher is usually speaking in the morning soon after his breakfast and before the equilibrium of his waking day has been firmly established. Then his task of the moment is not only to address an audience, but also to officiate at a liturgical function of which the sermon is one part. He does not have the lecturer's advantage, for instance, of walking slowly to a platform, seating himself, listening to a chairman's introduction, and then rising to applause. He must turn abruptly from his liturgical function to the business of public speaking. His particular audience, too, is not always the most ideal one for a public speaker. These people have not come to church expressly to hear him speak: They have not read advance notices about his talk, nor have they paid an admission fee for his lecture; indeed, in most cases they have no knowledge of who the preacher will be at the particular Mass they are attending. They listen politely and encouragingly, but they have no advance involvement in his talk; they are not waiting expectantly for him to speak.

In addition, the preacher's listeners are not always in the most advantageous mood for a serious message. They, too, are usually in attendance at a morning service and it is Sunday morning. Their day lies before them with all the particular rituals of Sunday in America: the visiting relatives, the Sunday dinner, the golf game, the trip to the country. The listener is often preoccupied: What time is grandmother going to arrive? Do I have enough roast for the whole crowd? I wonder if the brakes in the car are tight enough for a trip to the mountains? If I get out of here by eleven o'clock, I can be on the golf course by noon. These ideas are swirling in their minds as they sit back to hear your message. They have not come in the same mood they would have if they were attending a lecture; they have not expressly segregated this time to hear a serious talk. They have come to church, and during this service they will hear you talk. They will be here for forty-five minutes, and then they will rush back to pick up the rhythm of their Sunday lives. In fact, during the wintertime they sit there bundled in their overcoats (most churches do not have the advantage of a cloakroom), and this only compounds the transient, unsettled mood, as if they were all prepared to dash away and would do so at a moment's notice.

Nor are the physical arrangements any less discouraging. The average church does not have the settled, comfortable feeling of a lecture hall where the doors are firmly closed when the talk begins and everyone watches the speaker. In a church during Sunday Mass there are busy little activities going on all the time: the latecomers who push in and out of pews; the ushers collecting their baskets in the rear of the church; the members of the choir riffling through books to find the next hymn; and the inevitable crying children. Outside the church the situation is even more dispiriting—the parking lot is filled with cars, rows and rows of them, and they must be cleared ten minutes before the next Mass so the new herd of cars can take their places. The preacher has forty-five minutes to complete the entire service and get these people back in that parking lot. The whole atmosphere is hardly conducive to a relaxed, careful discussion of some serious theme.

So disconcerting is the situation—the rushed preacher, the transient audience, and the unsettled atmosphere—that many preachers develop a serious disaffection for Sunday preaching. It becomes for them vexatious, annoying, and deeply unsatisfying. Often they prefer other and more calm preaching situations: evening devotions, organization meetings, after-dinner talks. The Sunday sermon is therefore performed perfunctorily and with dispatch—an annoying task to be gotten rid of quickly. Perhaps this is one reason that Sunday sermons are so often done poorly: It just does not seem worth the effort.

But what a tragic mistake if a preacher allows himself to fall into that attitude. What a dereliction of duty. This man has been commissioned by the Lord to be the *keryx*, the herald of the good news, and the people of God are seated before him to hear the message. How sad if he allows the difficulties of the situation to overwhelm him.

The assembly of Christians on the Sabbath is the ordinary occasion for the herald to perform his duty. The priest, of course, is to announce the good news of Jesus whenever he has an opportunity; but, as we indicated in Part I, the Sunday sermon is the only realistic and continuing opportunity for the church to speak to her people. Other preaching situations might be more glamorous, more intriguing, and more flattering, but they merely involve fractional segments of the body Catholic. One modern commentator calls Sunday preaching "the priest's bread-and-butter preaching," and so it is: the place where he encounters the people of God, the continuing occasion for announcing the good news, the moment when he does his job.

The difficulties inherent in Sunday preaching should only drive the preacher to a more careful examination of his task, and a more diligent self-preparation. Even more than other public speakers, the preacher must master the techniques outlined in Part I of this book. He must regain his poise and take charge of the audience by means of our principles: desire, command, communication, preparation. He must discover his best voice, then develop it through the ASRM principle. He must speak in the Conversational Mode with modulation, vocal variety, gestures, and projection. The problems of the Sunday preaching experience should not dishearten the preacher; they should only goad him on to the mastery of the Art of Public Speaking. It can be accomplished easily enough, as we indicated in Part I.

But fundamentally the preacher should remind himself that he is the herald of the word. The liturgical renewal commissioned by Vatican II has brought this role into sharper focus by ritual changes in the liturgy itself. Changes in the Mass now clearly indicate the twofold service that is taking place: the liturgy of the word and the liturgy of the Eucharist. The liturgy of the word (the early part of the Mass up to the offertory) is a continuation of the Old Testament synagogue service at which the Scriptures were read and explained. When Jesus established the new kingdom of God, the original type of synagogue service was retained, and to it was added a eucharistic service, a continuation of the Lord's Last Supper. We now, therefore, have two services at one occasion, and the new rubrics of our time delineate that quite clearly.

When the early church continued the traditional synagogue service as part of the new rite, it retained the two elements of the liturgy of the word: reading from the sacred texts and preaching. But a new dimension was added to the preaching of the word, something clearly indicated in St. Paul's epistles: The word of the new kingdom was dynamic and contained a real efficacy; it was an occasion at which God communicated some kind of grace (i.e., *charis*). The preaching of this word is presented as something that "fructifies and develops . . . a divine power for the salvation of every believer . . . living and efficient and keener than any two-edged sword." Thus St. Paul's farewell to the Elders of Ephesus as recounted in the Acts:

> And now I commend you to the Lord and to the word of his grace which has the power to build up and to give the inheritance among all the sanctified.

Or as he writes to the Thessalonians:

> And for this reason, we too as well as you thank God continually, namely, because when you had received from us the word which you heard, God's word, you welcomed it, not as a human word but, as it really is, a word of God which also is made operative in you who believe.

We leave it to the professional theologians to determine the precise modality of this grace; we are only concerned with the fact of the reality: that preaching the word is an operation in the area of God's grace, that the preacher is somehow an instrument of grace. He preaches the word, which fructifies and develops and is living and efficient and has power and is operative. Two obvious conclusions flow from this. First, the preacher is working in the area of grace, something quite holy and serious, and he therefore cannot afford to be perfunctory and unconcerned about his Sunday preaching. And second, he is an instrument of this power (since certainly the word does not confer grace *ex opere operato*, as do the sacraments) and he must make himself as fit and useful an instrument as

possible, utilizing all the techniques of public speaking and persuasiveness we outlined earlier.

The *Constitution on the Liturgy* from Vatican II prescribes that a
homily be preached every Sunday; and then it outlines the dimensions of kerygmatic preaching, the kind of preaching we have been
advocating in this book. Discussing the content of the sermon, the
Constitution states that the homily should explain "either some aspect of the readings from Holy Scripture or of another text from the
Ordinary or Proper of the Mass of the day, taking into account the
mystery which is being celebrated and the particular needs of
the hearers." This is a biblically oriented form of preaching since
the content of the preacher's sermon should come either from the
Scriptures themselves or from the liturgy, which is composed
chiefly of Scripture. The *Constitution* also states that the character
of the homily "should be that of a proclamation of God's wonderful
works in the history of salvation, the mystery of Christ, ever made
present within us, especially in the celebration of the liturgy."
And this, of course, is a dynamic, vital, enthusiastic kind of preaching.

"Holy Scripture." "The particular needs of the hearers." "A proclamation of God's wonderful works." These are the key concepts of
the *Constitution's* directives about preaching. And they can be summarized in the one word kerygmatic—preaching that proclaims the
good news enthusiastically.

The word "homily," however, requires a few words of explanation, especially for those who are not accustomed to this form of
preaching. The homily was the traditional form of preaching in the
early church, and it consisted fundamentally of an explanation of
some selected section of Scripture and then an application of the
message to the audience. This was a broad concept, and it admitted
a variety of different kinds of sermon, all included under the basic
category of the homily. The essential characteristic of the homily
was the fact that the message was based on the good news as it was
found in Scripture. The contemporary preacher should not con-
fine himself to a narrow interpretation of the homily and thus expose
himself to the danger of preaching sermons that are pedantic line-
by-line examinations of biblical texts, sermons that would be tedious
and oppressively boring. The purpose of the preaching directives
in the *Constitution* is to underscore the preacher's role as herald of
the good news and to insist that he exercise that role during the

liturgy of the word at the Christian assembly on the Sabbath. But the homily must, at all costs, be 1) interesting, 2) diversified, and 3) relevant. Let us examine these requirements.

1. *Interesting.* The preacher needs to take the good news as it is presented in the particular section of Scripture that the liturgy offers and then make it attractive for his audience. It would be deadly if every Sunday sermon began with the words: "In this morning's gospel we see the story of . . ." The preacher must use all the techniques of introduction and conclusion we discussed earlier, and he must also use the methods we outlined for making a sermon interesting. He needs to select fresh and vigorous language, supply illustrations, and use occasional emotion. The homily requires all the techniques of good public speaking.

A homily is not a technical exegesis of Scripture; it is only a popular, but intelligent presentation of the scriptural message. Thus the preacher could either cite the Scripture at the beginning of his sermon, or in the middle, or at the end. Sometimes he might want to follow the text of the Scripture closely throughout the course of the entire sermon. Example: the parable of the sower and the seed (Sexagesima Sunday)—here the preacher could follow the parable of Jesus to describe the four categories of the Christian life. Again at other times he might only quote the central statement from a passage of Scripture. Example: The parable of the weeds sown among the wheat (5th Sunday after Epiphany)—here the preacher might only quote the statement of the owner that he did not want to destroy the weeds because he would simultaneously have to kill the good seed; and from that he could proceed into a discussion of moral evil in the world. In fact, he could begin his sermon with the sharp statement, "Did you ever wonder why God allows evil and malice in his world—a dictator, wars, race hatred?" and then continue to explore that question until he arrives at the solution presented by Jesus in the parable. At other times the preacher might simply employ the general theme of a section of Scripture without analyzing any specific text. Example: The parable of the mustard seed (6th Sunday after Epiphany)—here the preacher could quote Jesus' statement that the kingdom of heaven must develop like the mustard seed that grows into a large plant, and then inaugurate a discussion of our obligation to help the kingdom grow and spread. At other times the preacher might only use one phrase from a longer section of Scripture for the theme of his sermon. Example: St. Paul's advice to the Ephesians that they should "follow the way of love" (Epistle for 3rd Sunday in Lent)—here the preacher could use this one statement as a prelude to a discussion that the Christian message is basically one of love, love of God and our brothers.

Whatever the particular passage of Scripture the priest is discussing, he must first study the possible ways of presentation. He must ask himself how he can create the greatest amount of audience impact and how he can best engage his listeners. The preacher must preach the good news from the pages of the Scriptures—but he must make it interesting, or his audience will not listen.

2. *Diversified.* The *Constitution* requires the preacher to base his sermon on the liturgical texts, and that is fine because it guarantees that he will keep his message close to the basic good news. There is a danger, however, that a preacher might not diversify his selection and thus preach the same sermon on the same Sunday year after year. If, for instance, the preacher speaks about the parable of the mustard seed on the sixth Sunday after Epiphany one year, he should not repeat the same sermon to the same congregation on that Sunday the following year(s). Parishioners, particularly those in a small parish, immediately recognize the yearly sermon and are annoyed and bored because of the preacher's failure to employ some imagination and creativity. The liturgy of the sixth Sunday after Epiphany, for example, contains more than the story of the mustard seed. The Epistle suggests a number of themes and topics: "the constancy of your hope fixed on our Lord Jesus Christ"; "beloved brothers of God, we know how you have been chosen"; "you became imitators . . . of the Lord"; "joy that comes from the Holy Spirit"; "to serve the living and true God and to await the coming down from heaven of his Son whom he raised from the dead, Jesus, who delivers us from the wrath to come." The Offertory: "The right hand of the Lord has struck with power: the right hand of the Lord has exalted me; I shall not die, but live and declare the works of the Lord." The Communion Verse: "All marveled at the words that came from the mouth of God." The Postcommunion: "We beseech you that we may ever hunger after those things by which we truly live." There are enough good topics in the liturgy of this one Sunday for a dozen sermons. The preacher, therefore, must employ his ingenuity to present different facets of the good news.

3. *Relevant.* The preacher should develop his homily according to the FERM principle, and that, of course, includes the element of

relevancy. The *Constitution* notes two aspects of that relevancy as it pertains to the Sunday audience. First, it speaks of "the mystery of Christ, ever made present and active within us." This implies that we are preaching about the risen, living Christ, not an abstract, historical Christ who lived two thousand years ago. The preacher's task, as we indicated in the preceding chapter, is to present the person of Jesus to the audience—as He is at this very moment: risen in heaven, but also united and joined to the Christian listener in your audience. The preacher must present to his listeners the Jesus he knows—in line with what Thomas Carlyle told his pastor: "What the church needs are men who know God by more than hearsay." The ultimate point of the good news is that Jesus is risen, living, and *here*. That is the way the preacher must speak of Him.

Second, the *Constitution* speaks of Christ as present and active "especially in the celebration of the liturgy." And it also says that the homilies should preserve "the intimate connection with at least the principal seasons of the liturgical year." Each year the church relives the life of Jesus in the celebration of its liturgy, and the preacher should recall that element of relevancy in his homily. During the advent season, we recall the waiting and yearning of the human race for the Christ; then at the Christmas season, the overwhelming good news of the Incarnation, God with us; in Lent and Passiontide, the moving fact of our redemption, Jesus' offering himself for us; then the Paschal victory, Jesus' resurrection and ours. To recall the Christian moment of worship is to achieve more complete relevancy.

When the preacher prepares his homily for the people of God on Sunday morning, he must retain all the effective techniques of good contemporary public speaking. He must take special effort to make his homily interesting, diversified, and relevant.

For the reader who has followed the plan of this book thus far, the *Constitution* performs the service of localizing at the moment of Sunday worship all the things we have been discussing. The document underscores the importance of Sunday preaching and its intimate relationship with the act of worship—it states: "The homily, therefore, is to be highly esteemed as a part of the liturgy itself." The priest is to be the minister of the word, as well as the minister of the Eucharist, and he should neglect neither office.

Despite the inherent difficulties of the Sunday preaching experience—the early hour, the transient listeners sitting in their over-coats, the noisy latecomers, the busy ushers, the distracted choir members, the crying child, the jammed parking lot—the priest must still function as the herald of the good news. He is involved in a moment of grace, announcing the word, which fructifies and has power and is operative. But he must make himself as efficient an instrument as possible: He must practice all the techniques we have outlined for developing his best voice, for using the conversational mode, for achieving persuasiveness, for making his sermon interesting. That is his duty as a herald.

As the priest examines his role in society at this time of Christian renewal, he often begins to analyze and categorize the various activities in which he is engaged. So many of these activities, he concludes, have little connection with his apostolic mission and yet they occupy a major part of his time—fund raising, for instance, and supervision of buildings, plant management, purchasing, planning of construction, financing, and coaching athletic teams. Consequently there has been much discussion about the advisability of drawing laymen more closely into the operation of the church so that they can make their unique contribution in these areas where they have proficiency, so that the priest can spend more time on those things that are more closely related to his apostolate. Whatever the advisability or practicality of that, it remains quite evident the priest's role as herald of the good news should not be compromised by these other activities, nor can it be accomplished by laymen. This is the priest's unique office; and if he does not fulfill it when he steps into the pulpit on Sunday morning, no one else can do it for him, and—unhappily!—the good news will not be announced to the people of God.

EXERCISES

• Remember: The assembly of Christians on the Sabbath is the ordinary occasion where the herald of the good news performs his function, and the difficulties of the situation should not deter him from his duty.

• Remember: The herald is working in the area of grace, preaching the word, which fructifies and has power and is efficient; but this does not exonerate him from the demands of good public speaking: to the contrary, he must make himself a fit instrument for this important moment.

• Remember: The homily is traditionally an explanation of some selected section of Scripture with an application of the message to the audience.

• Remember: The contemporary homily must retain the essential characteristic of a scripturally based message that is made relevant to the audience; but it must also be:

1. *Interesting.*
   • Do not begin every sermon: "In this morning's gospel we see the story of . . ."
   • Quote the Scripture either at the beginning, or in the middle, or at the end.
   • Sometimes follow the line of the scriptural story closely (e.g., parable of the sower and the seed).
   • At other times simply quote a central passage (e.g., parable of the weeds and the wheat).
   • Or sometimes only employ the general theme of the passage of Scripture (e.g., parable of the mustard seed).
   • Or use just one phrase from a longer section of Scripture (e.g., St. Paul's "follow the way of love" in Ephesians 5, 2).

2. *Diversified.*
   • Do not preach the same sermon to the same congregation on the same day year after year.
   • Diversify your material: The *Constitution* allows the preacher to select his topic from any part of the liturgy.
   • Review our example in this chapter of the potential material in the liturgy for the sixth Sunday after Epiphany.

3. *Relevant.*
   • Preach Jesus as risen, living, present—and personal and immediate to each one of your listeners.
   • Preach Jesus in the liturgical context of the ecclesiastical year.

By way of review: Coordinate the elements of this part of the book (the good news, the use of Scripture, and the homily) with the techniques of public speaking and persuasiveness:

Make sure that your homily is:
1. Preached in your best voice (The ASRM principle).
2. Spoken in the Conversational Mode—
   • Modulation (No monotone).

• Vocal Variety (Vary your rate of speed and volume; force an occasional point; create a magic moment by a pause).
• Pace (Use vocal commas to achieve proper tempo).
• Gestures (Create the impulse to gesture).
• Projection (Hit that back wall).

3. *Persuasive.*

• Organize your homily under one thesis—remember: If you cannot summarize your homily in a one-sentence thesis, it is too vague for your audience to follow.
• Develop your homily according to the FERM principle:
  • Facts (Get the issue on the board).
  • Explanation (Beware of the preacher's *patella*).
  • Relevancy (Keep one leg off the ground).
  • Motivation (Get your listeners to say "Yes, yes.")

4. *Interesting.*

• Use stories to create audience interest (Remember the tower of Siloe).
• Employ fresh and colorful language (Recall Jesus' attractive phraseology).
• Occasionally appeal to your listeners' emotions (Recall Kitty Genovese).

4

SITUATION PREACHING

In addition to his regular Sunday preaching, the priest is frequently given the opportunity to address other groups in other situations. These experiences in situation preaching not only afford the preacher the opportunity of preaching the good news more extensively, but they also provide him with the advantage of being able to create greater relevancy for the audience he is addressing. The sermon in church on Sunday must, of necessity, be addressed to a heterogeneous group composed of people of different age groups and different sex, people of different educational backgrounds, cultural levels, and economic status, and even different stages of spiritual development. The preacher must communicate the good news to the group he sees before him in the church—to the old lady in the front pew, to the teen-age boy to his right, to the young mother on his left, to the businessman over there, to the old man in the back row. This requires that he say things that are somehow relevant to all the people in his audience. But situation preaching often presents the preacher with a more homogeneous group— whether it be a youth group, or a men's organization, or a ladies' organization, or a group of religious, or what have you. And he then has the splendid opportunity of relating the good news a little more closely to the actual situation and condition of his listeners.

When the preacher prepares his remarks for one of these special groups, he should keep the character of the group in mind and attempt to make his statements as relevant and practical as possible for this particular group. If he does not, he is missing a magnificent opportunity for increased audience contact. If a man prepares a talk on Christian joy and then gives that exact same talk without any modification or adaptation to a group of cloistered nuns, a teen-age club, a Rotary luncheon, a ladies' sodality meeting, a communion breakfast for the Holy Name Society, a group of nurses, and a group of grammar school children, he is not addressing himself to the needs and situation and mentality of each group. He is not realistically relevant.

This does not imply that a preacher must preach some different kind of Christianity to each one of these groups. The good news of Jesus offers the same message for all people, but it must be applied and actuated by each individual in his own situation. And when a preacher speaks to a group that is somehow homogeneous, he can then direct his remarks to that situation.

Here are three quick and efficient rules for the preacher who is preparing a talk for a situation group:

1. Think of the precise character of the group.
2. Think of the group's problems.
3. Think of the group's Christian potentialities.

The three rules offer the preacher a quick and sure avenue into the real condition of his situation group. The preacher should, first, recall the precise and actual character of his group. If, for example, he is speaking to a group of student nurses, he should think of the student nurse's situation: the hospital, the long hours of training, the patients, the supervisors, bandages, blood, operations, death, her fellow nurses, the necessary spirit of dedication. Now he has a precise picture of the group. That talk on Christian joy, which he might be presenting without any modification to a variety of different groups, should be somewhat related to this group of people who work in hospitals, assist at operations, and see death almost daily.

Secondly, the preacher should consider the realistic and precise problems that this group encounters—problems perhaps that no other group experiences. The nurse's problem might be one of fatigue and weariness in ministering to the sick. Or impatience, as she has to deal with cranky and querulous patients. Or adjustment to authority, as she has to submit to imprudent and unrealistic demands of her supervisors. Or a growing insensitivity and coldness towards the problems of the sick. Or a struggle to maintain her high ideals in the real work-a-day world of the hospital. These are the problems to which the preacher could direct his material.

Thirdly, he should consider the Christian potentialities of the group, the ideals they could possibly achieve in their situation. The nurse in her situation has an enviable opportunity to serve Christ in the person of her patients. She can make her patients more whole —physically and emotionally and spiritually—by her joy, her compassion, and her service. She can be a witness to Jesus by the very tenor of her life, by the things she says, by the things she does. If she is faithful to the ideals of her profession, she can ennoble herself and become a mature, compassionate, attractive person. These are some of the goals and objectives that the preacher could suggest to his listeners.

The preacher can obtain the information he needs to understand his group's character, problems, and potential from a variety of sources. He might be able to recall this information from his own personal experience, or he could consult people who have had some experience with the group he is going to address, or he could do some research in books and magazine articles. The information is available, but the preacher must have the interest and enthusiasm and sense of personal responsibility to search for it. His audience deserves that much attention.

If the preacher employs these three simple rules, he will discover that he is achieving insight into the group, and he can then present his message of the good news as it is directly related to the people in this group. And his listeners will say: "He is talking to *us*. He really understands us."

Here are three actual incidents involving three different priests who had to employ their ingenuity in situational preaching episodes. These episodes are somewhat unusual and perhaps will not be encountered frequently by the average preacher, but they serve to illustrate the dynamics of situational preaching.

1. A priest was invited to conduct a day of recollection for a group of seventy-five doctors' wives. As he was preparing his material, he wondered whether he could discover anything particularly relevant to this group or whether he should simply preach the good news without any attempt at application. He consulted some people who had acquaintance with the medical profession and discovered that a fairly common problem of doctors' wives is their sense of loneliness in their affluence. Physicians provided extremely well for their families, but the demands of their profession—the great expenditure of time, the mental preoccupation, and sometimes even the emotional preoccupation—projected their wives into a state of

loneliness and a feeling that they were only sharing a minimal part of their husbands' time and interest. The preacher addressed himself to that problem, explaining the demands of love and Christian compassion; he discussed his listeners' problem and tried to offer some solution, or at least some enlightenment and understanding of it. The women's reaction at the end of the day was one of deep gratitude for a helpful and satisfying day—and also a reaction of wonder and pleasant surprise that this priest should understand them so well.

2. A pastor had trained a new group of altar boys and was about to start them on their regular assignments on the altar. But he had devised a brief investiture ceremony in the church at which he formally presented each boy with his cassock and surplice. He invited another priest to give a talk at this investiture service. A problem: What do you say to a group of new altar boys? Tell them to show up on time? Comb their hair? Shine their shoes? Stay awake on the altar? All this sounded a bit trite, and so the priest began to consider other possibilities and came up with this unusual turn: he looked up the ancient service for the investiture of a knight in the medieval age and recounted some of its main features to the altar boys—the selection, the vigil, the knight's promise, his commitment to honor. Then he compared the altar boy to the knight, showing how he too was a privileged and selected person and how he had a commitment to honor and duty and dignity. The boys followed the preacher with close attention as he outlined the importance and dignity of the tasks they were being given. Had the preacher merely recounted a tired list of do's and don't's, his listeners would have squirmed in their seats and said to themselves: "Another lecture from teacher."

3. Another priest was invited to conduct a retreat at a men's college that had an unhappy record of past retreats. There was a rule at the college that all the men had to attend the opening talk of the retreat, but attendance for the remainder of the retreat was optional. The result was that the college chapel was crowded with students for the opening talk, but almost deserted for the remainder of the time. An average of no more than ten percent of the students had been attending the retreats. Here was the preacher's problem: he had one opportunity to reach these men and make them stay with him for the remainder of the retreat; but if he lost them at the opening talk, they were gone for good. He decided to

attempt something drastic, something that should be employed very rarely and very judiciously. At the close of that first talk he asked all the men in the crowded chapel to take a good look at the man sitting directly to their right. The men smiled, shrugged, and looked to their right. Then the priest asked them to look at the man on their left. Then the man directly in front of them. And finally the man directly behind them. When the men had quieted down again, he said: "The reason I asked you to take a good look at those fellows was because you won't be seeing them here any more during the retreat. And the reason you won't be seeing them is because of something you didn't notice when you looked at them, something you couldn't see. Each one of those fellows has a big yellow streak running right down his back. He's too yellow and doesn't have enough guts to come here all week and hear the things Christ wants him to do. Pray for that guy with the yellow streak. He needs it." The reaction was one of stunned silence. But the attendance at that retreat was close to a hundred percent. The priest stayed up until two and three o'clock in the morning talking to the men individually. They formed in long lines outside his room, and one night he was unable to get to bed at all. When his car pulled away from the campus, they surrounded it cheering. They could not get enough of this priest who knew how to talk to men.

These incidents, as we stated, are somewhat unusual, but they do demonstrate the efforts some preachers take to reach their group in a situational preaching episode. They thought about the group, they considered the group's problems and its potential. In every situational preaching episode the preacher should have a similar urgency to reach the group.

Let us now briefly discuss four preaching situations that priests frequently do encounter: preaching to children, preaching to teen-agers, parish missions, and retreats. Our purpose is not to engage in a full discussion of all the mechanics of these situations, but simply to underscore a few aspects of the dynamics of situational preaching as related to these groups.

1. PREACHING TO CHILDREN.

Speaking to children is a true test of an adult's own personal maturity. Many people become extremely self-conscious and artificial when speaking to children and consequently do not communicate. Others become highly paternalistic with a "Tut tut, my dear child" and a pat on the head, and they do not communicate either. Only the mature person who is in control and has command of himself can communicate with children in the proper way—that is, speaking to them as *persons*. Granted, children are immature, inexperienced, growing, not fully developed—but they are still persons and should be addressed as persons. This demands that the preacher approach them with interest in them, with honesty, with forthrightness, and with a realization of their limitations and present state of development. And that is the test of the speaker's maturity: his ability to communicate with these perons who are not as developed as he is and yet do it without becoming either self-conscious or overbearing.

A short time ago, I requested some mothers and educators to ask their children of grammar school age a question about preaching to children. The actual question: "How do you like the priest to preach to you from the pulpit?" The question is somewhat imprecise, but I wanted the children's immediate and nonreflective answer to this leading question. Here are the verbatim, unedited answers to the question: "How do you like the priest to preach to you from the pulpit?":

Casual, and not stiff.

I don't think it is very nice, and I don't like it when a priest reads without looking up at me.

Nice and gentle and smooth.

I like him to give an example to explain his point.

Funny.

In a nice way.

I like to see a priest get excited.

Not too solemn.

Don't preach to me, but talk to me.

I like to hear a priest preach sermons on the gospel, because I don't understand the gospel when it is read.

Talking directly to me, sort of person-to-person.

Not so long that you get bored and squirmy.

I like the gospels—I guess it's in the gospel about Christ standing on the water.

Nice.

I like him to tell a few jokes.

These candid answers from the children might offer many insights about the situational aspect of preaching to children, but the principal thing they demonstrate is that these children are persons who have very determined ideas about how the priest should preach to them. Thus the preacher cannot contact them when he allows himself to become either self-conscious or overbearing. These little people are persons—and they want to be talked to as persons.

We might here formulate three precise rules which could serve as a rule of thumb for the preacher when he addresses a group of children:

1. Do not talk down to them.
2. Talk to them in their language.
3. Employ the technique of question and story.

The first rule underscores our original point that children are persons. Therefore the preacher should not speak down to them; he should speak to them directly and immediately, as one person talking to another. This demands honesty and candor and a forthright attitude on the part of the preacher.

The second rule reminds the preacher of the necessity of speaking to children in their language. He should, of course, avoid the platitudinous vocabulary of "necessary dispositions" and "voluntary acts"—even adults do not understand that. But he must also be careful that his vocabulary be not too involved or elevated: He is speaking to people who are at a lower level of education. However, the preacher must not make the opposite mistake of underestimating the vocabulary of children and thus talk to them in an artificial "itsey-bitsey-coo" language. If the preacher wants to learn the level of children's vocabulary, let him listen to them speak, and let him peruse some of their text books. He might be surprised.

The third rule suggests the two unfailing ways to capture children's attention: questions and stories. Instead of preaching a direct message to the children, the preacher could engage in the technique of asking them questions, and thus leading them through his material. He might even leave the pulpit and stand in the aisle closer to the children. Ask simple questions, leading questions, funny questions. But—a vitally important point—do not designate any particular child and make him give an answer. Let the children volunteer answers, otherwise you might create a tense atmosphere and make your sermon seem like an examination. In this technique, the children and the preacher are immediately involved together in the sermon.

Children, like their parents, enjoy stories and follow them intently. However, the story must not be too involved or sophisticated. The gospel stories are direct and easy to comprehend. Incidents from the life of Jesus are appealing to the children. And the lives of the saints, if they are recounted simply and intelligently, offer attractive material for the young child. Tell them a good story and they will listen.

Speaking to children is a somewhat demanding enterprise, but if it is mastered it can be an extremely satisfying and rewarding experience. The reactions of children are frank and candid and quite moving. Jesus experienced this when he gathered the children on his lap and talked to them in a person-to-person manner.

2. PREACHING TO TEEN-AGERS.

Many priests find that preaching to teen-agers is a disappointing experience. The teen-agers sit in the pews and listen politely, but what the preacher says seems to have so little impact on their lives. Much of the preacher's problem in communicating with teen-agers derives from a failure to recognize the situational aspect of preaching to this group.

First of all, the preacher should recognize the precise situation of a teen-ager. The teen-ager is neither child nor adult—he is an adolescent, or even a young adult. Some preachers make the mistake of speaking to teen-agers as if they were young children, and, therefore, they do not communicate because these adolescents are not young children. Other preachers pay no attention to the precise situation of the teen-agers and address them as if they were an adult group, and they fail to communicate because these adolescents are not adults either. The answer, of course, is for the preacher to address himself directly to the teen-agers' actual situation in twentieth century America.

There are many facets to the modern teen-ager's situation and mentality, but there are three principal characteristics that peculiarly identify him as an adolescent of this time: bewilderment, inquisitiveness, and generosity.

1. Bewilderment. The modern adolescent enters into the contemporary scene in a state of bewilderment. He was born in a time of cold war, a time when the destruction of our civilization could come hurtling from the sky at any moment. He sees rank injustices in our society and the deprivation of basic civil liberties and decencies. He did not make this world—he inherited it from his forebears. And he feels cheated and defrauded because we have done such a bad job with the world. He is, therefore, only too ready to reject existing forms and categories and methods—they do not work, he says, and he wants to try something new. This is one of the root causes of his disaffection for obedience, for following the paths we have trod.

2. Inquisitiveness. The modern teen-ager has at his disposal more facts and data than any other adolescent in history. These facts are unassimilated and unformulated, and he has no particular insight into them; but he does possess these facts. He has broken down the habitual barriers to adolescent information: he can see anything, read anything, get in his car and in a few minutes be miles away from his home and city—he has discovered the world at a younger age. Thus he is not at all ready to accept and believe something merely because another man says it is so, whether that man be parent or teacher or preacher. He wants reasons for everything. He will believe, but we have to tell him why.

3. Generosity. Today's teen-ager has a fantastic amount of potential generosity, an exciting spirit of dedication. He is the youth who may join the Peace Corps, enlist in causes, dedicate himself to working for the betterment of society. But he has to believe in the cause.

This teen-ager, this bewildered, inquisitive, generous adolescent is the person who sits before you listening to your words. He wants you to understand him, and if he feels that you do not understand him he will reject your message. Someone has written that the two magical words in a counseling situation are: "I understand." If a person feels that you understand, then the avenue of communication is immediately opened. The teen-ager needs this sense of understanding from the preacher. If he feels that you are thinking, "These kids are all crazy today," he will not listen to you. If he feels that you are only carping and criticizing without offering him any encouragement he will keep you at arm's length.

The content of the preacher's message should be the basic good news. We must tell these adolescents that God is real and that He loves them and wants their love in return. The preacher must, of course, present the person of Christ, and that means it must be the real Christ, and not the ethereal, somewhat effeminate Christ of the holy card. It is particularly important that the preacher present a virile and imitable Christ to teen-age boys; he must show that Jesus was a real man: He worked in a carpenter shop; He spent His ministry hiking over the countryside; He slept outdoors on the ground wrapped in His cloak; He was whipped and nailed to the wood of the cross without cry or whimper. Jesus is a real man, a hero to follow.

All five aspects of the good news must be preached to teen-agers. They must be shown that the good news has impact on their whole lives and that religion is not just a sacristy experience, a pie-in-the-sky philosophy. Prayer is realistic contact with the living Jesus and not merely a monotonous recitation of rote formulae. We are called to Christian commitment in contemporary society, dedication to the needs of all men. We are to love everybody, not merely by putting pennies in a mission box, but by real and tangible acts of love.

A recent survey taken among graduates of Catholic high schools posed the question: "What is more important for a Catholic—love of your neighbor, or abstaining from meat on Friday?" Fifty-three percent answered that love of neighbor was more important, while the other forty-seven percent said that abstinence from meat was more important. Almost half of those graduates felt that abstinence was more important than love! Somebody had not been getting the Christian message through to those adolescents.

The preacher should explain sin to the adolescent as unfaithfulness to Jesus. During the years of adolescence, the teen-ager is experiencing the stirrings and blooming of his sexual faculties, and he thereby discovers new difficulties in faithfulness to the Lord. The preacher must explain the naturalness of these stirrings and the inherent beauty of sex. But he must show that sex is a wonderful and private affair between two married people. He must be careful that his preaching does not degenerate into a pansexualism, with constant reminders about chastity that convey the impression that religion is equated with sexual abstinence.

And these teen-agers should be reminded that they are living
in the historical moment of the risen Jesus. They are to be involved
with the living Christ and their brothers here in the kingdom of God,
a community that has begun to live the resurrection. The preacher
can appeal to their generosity and their dedication, urging them to
become committed to Jesus and their brothers, showing them that
religion is a vital burning thing, a lifelong experience that is exciting
and satisfying.

These young men and women sitting in the pews, these adolescents of today present a challenging task for the preacher. These
young people are bewildered and inquisitive and generous—a much
more complicated group than that of previous generations. But if
the preacher can communicate with them he can accomplish something of tremendous importance—he can make them the enlight-
ened and dedicated Christian adults of tomorrow.

3. PARISH MISSIONS.

Is the parish mission obsolete? An unhealthy remnant of a mis-
guided preaching tradition? A creaky device that has no place in
the renewed church? These are the questions that are being asked
today, and they deserve serious attention.

The critics of the parish mission point to the traditional structure
of the mission as we have known it for the past seventy-five years
in our country, and the picture that emerges is not a happy one.
The fiery sermons about hell and judgment. The thumping oratory
about the sanctity of the marriage bed. The tired jokes. The easy
clichés. The mechanical presentation of "the means of salvation."
The unmistakable flavor of that old time religion. The sawdust trail.
Billy Sunday urging the sinners to come forth. Cotton Mather
breathing threats about the licking flames of hell. Elmer Gantry
pounding his pulpit.

But despite all of that there was one element that was essentially
healthy and valuable—the sense of spiritual renewal in the parish
during the time of the mission. It was something reminiscent of
what St. Paul did on his third missionary journey when he visited
the Christian communities, comforting them, strengthening them in
the faith, instructing them. St. Luke writes of one such episode:

> And as he wanted to go to Achaia, the brethren en-
> couraged him and wrote to the disciples to welcome

him. On his arrival there he was of great service to those who had believed.

But there is a tremendous difference between the apostle coming to herald the good news to the Christian community and the Billy Sunday experience. How did the apostolic mission degenerate into the old sawdust trail? Probably as a result of the infiltration of the unfortunate preaching traditions we mentioned earlier. The Redemptorist Paul Hitz, a member of the Pastoral Center of Home Missions in Paris, has written an incisive critique of the parish mission that underscores this problem:

> On the whole, I should say that modern mission preaching continues to hand on the true elements of the Christian message, but in a perspective very different from, and far poorer than, that of the New Testament. Its cardinal point, its central vision, is far too much man and what he does, not primarily and simultaneously God's action to save us in Christ. Hence this misplaced stress, this warping of the perspective, that we find in mission preaching as a whole and in every individual sermon, making them, in comparison with the revelation of the New Testament, seem so much less Christian, less faithful to the Gospel. This explains the unfortunate impression which traditional mission preaching makes upon so many really well-intentioned people, upon splendid Christians of our time . . . Ten years or so ago, a young priest (member of a mission institute) took part in a city mission which was certainly well-preached. He had later to make this admission: "After the evening sermons I did my New Testament reading, and could not help feeling what a difference there was between it and what we do!" . . . During one large city mission, some years ago, a priest, professor in a Catholic institute, reflected: "Either the Bible and liturgy need to be completely reformed, or else these sermons are not really Christian."

The problem, then, is basically our old one: a failure to preach the good news. Other philosophies have distorted the Christian message out of focus—particularly Pelagianism, which makes the whole Christian life a heroic human effort; and moralism, which stresses out of proportion the moral aspects of the Christian message. The principal corrective measure, therefore, for whatever deformities exist in mission preaching consists in a preaching of the good news.

The parish mission, understood in the sense of the Pauline apostolic visit, can only confer enormous benefits upon a parish. It is a time of spiritual renewal, a time for gaining greater insight into the Christian message, a moment for Christian remotivation and rededication, a season of prayer, a Christian experience of the most authentic nature. The herald of the good news appears in the people's midst, he preaches the good news, he counsels the people, encourages them, and recommits them to the fullness of the Christian life. How extremely helpful this can be for a contemporary parish.

But the preacher must be the herald of the good news. He must be St. Paul and not Billy Sunday. He has to re-examine the Christian message as we outlined it earlier, and then preach all five aspects of it: Incarnational, Religious, Moral, Social, Eschatological. He should begin his course of sermons with the astonishing fact of God's love for us, His invitation to a life of union, and then proceed through the good news as it is related to a contemporary audience. This is far superior to the traditional mission program about the end of man, damnation, and the means of salvation—these are, of course, Christian themes, but their presentation and articulation are often out of focus, something picked from the good news and slightly distorted.

A number of new techniques are being submitted to experimentation during modern parish missions. Instead of the usual mission of services each evening for six nights, some parishes are conducting week-end missions: an intensified program in the parish throughout the entire day of Saturday and Sunday. Other parishes are conducting the Sunday Mass mission: mission services at the regular Sunday Masses for a period of four weeks. Others are conducting services on alternate nights, with special services for the various parish organizations. These techniques, and the other ones that are being devised, are all valuable—as long as they are predicated on the preaching of the good news.

St. Luke's statement about St. Paul in the Acts, which we quoted above, contains one other important point of insight for the contemporary mission: the preparation for the Apostolic visit—"And as he wanted to go to Achaia, the brethren encouraged him and wrote to the disciples to welcome him." A large part of the success of the parish spiritual renewal depends on the frame of mind of the parishioners, the amount of receptivity they possess, the way they have been prepared. Consequently many parishes today are embarking on extensive preparation programs for the parish mission—mail campaigns, telephone campaigns, door-to-door canvassing, posters and ads, announcements from the pulpit, constant reminders and explanations of the coming mission. All of this prepares the people for the mission, increases attendance, and greatly enhances the results. The mission can and should be one of the pivotal moments in the life of the parish, and it deserves adequate preparation and endeavor. One modern writer suggests that if each parish would only put into the parish mission an amount of community effort equal to that they muster in a fund raising campaign, then the parish would be renewed and revitalized.

These, then, are the three principal situational aspects for the contemporary preacher as he approaches the parish mission: a sense of parish renewal in the spirit of the Pauline visitation; the preaching of the good news; adequate preparation for the reception of the message. If the preacher can do that, then he will accomplish what St. Paul was able to do at Achaia—"He was of great service to those who had believed."

4. RETREATS.

The program, mechanics, method, and dynamics of a retreat constitute a major study in itself, something far beyond the scope and length of this book. Our purpose here is only to indicate some of the situational aspects of this particular preaching experience.

A retreat is a time of intensification of union between Jesus and the individual person. It is reminiscent of those scenes in the gospel when Jesus took the disciples aside for awhile to rest after a missionary journey: "Come apart into a desert place and rest awhile." And that section of Scripture contains the three principal characteristics of a retreat: the desert—the solitude and silence and reflective atmosphere during the time of the retreat; the rest—the period of re-establishment, of renewal for increased effort when one returns to his place in society; Jesus—the object of the retreat, the personal encounter with him.

Thus the preacher during a retreat should attempt to introduce each one of his listeners to Jesus in a more personal, more intimate way. And he should similarly attempt, in this time of solitude, to re-establish each one of his listeners in a greater commitment to Christ and his brothers. A retreat is a special time in a Christian's life, and the preacher should use this time wisely to accomplish these goals. Some retreat preachers do not always communicate this impression of a special time: they somehow communicate the idea that this retreat time is the right way to live, withdrawn, isolated, separated from the world; and consequently they separate the retreat from the total context of the Christian life and begin to preach a pietism and illuminism. Other retreat preachers allow the retreat to become a series of lectures or a compilation of moralisms, all flavored with a carefully selected number of incidents taken from lives of the saints. The retreat is none of these things: it is a moment of rest with Jesus which dynamizes the rest of the person's life.

The content of the preacher's message, of course, should be the basic good news, but now he has more time in which to develop it for his listeners. And if his retreat group has an homogeneous character—a group of priests, religious, youths, special categories of laymen—he can make his message particularly relevant to their needs according to the principles we outlined earlier in this chapter.

When the preacher addresses his retreat group he usually has a period of twenty-five to thirty minutes for each sermon, and thus he needs to arrange his material to fit that time span. He should employ the general principles of the FERM principle, but now he has the time for more precise explanation of some points, for a consideration of corollary material, for more use of illustrations. It is particularly necessary for the retreat preacher to make his material interesting because the retreatants are listening to a great deal of material, and if it is unmitigated fact after fact it can become extremely tedious. Humor, that precious human quality, can make its unique contribution toward an interesting and engaging talk.

A retreat to a group of religious should be approached with special attention and care. The good news of Jesus—all of it—should be preached with special vigor, because this basic Christian message has sometimes in some communities become clouded and distorted under the particular legislation of the community and by unhealthy ingredients of Latin and Gallic spirituality. The religious of today, more than ever, need the fresh and saving good news of Jesus. The preacher should also make that message relevant to the group within the framework of their particular commitment. He should address himself to the specific questions under discussion today: Maturity—the need to develop the spiritual and human personalities of the individual religious, the need to help them become healthy and responsible persons in the Christian world. Familial spirit—the necessity of creating a warm, human atmosphere in the community, with mutual love and respect and interest, making the community a home and not an institution. Authority—the problem of administration and honest initiative: the necessity of making administration loving and paternal, rather than cold and authoritarian; of respecting the good will and initiative of all members of the community; of organizing the goals of the community as a community project, and not just the private ideas of a few members; and the necessity of accepting a final decision with graciousness. Apostolate—the necessity for true apostolic engagement by the religious of today, recognizing it as a Christian imperative rather than a dangerous thing to be surrounded by cumbersome and artificial safeguards; the need to investigate and discover new forms and spheres for the Christian apostolate, and the corresponding need to consider the insights into the contemporary apostolate that any member of the community might offer.

Under the guidance of an intelligent and prudent herald of the good news, a retreatant can return to his particular place in society possessing a closer union with Jesus and a firmer commitment to his brothers; and he can be dynamized to live more consciously in this precise historical moment of the risen Jesus. That is no small value.

EXERCISES

• Remember: Situation preaching presents the preacher a unique opportunity for greater relevance.
• Remember the rules for situation preaching:
  1. Think of the precise character of the group.
  2. Think of the group's problems.
  3. Think of the group's Christian potentialities.

• Preaching to children:
  1. Do not talk down to them: talk to them as persons.
  2. Talk to them in their language.
  3. Employ the technique of question and story.

- Preaching to teen-agers:
  - Remember: You are dealing with an adolescent—neither child nor adult, but part of each.
  - Recall the main identifying characteristics of the modern adolescent—bewilderment, inquisitiveness, and generosity.
  - Show the teen-ager that you understand his condition.
  - Preach the good news to them—
    - Present Jesus as real and imitable and virile.
    - Show Christianity as a real and integrated part of their lives.
    - Present sin as unfaithfulness to Jesus, and do not descend into a pansexualism.
    - Enlist their spirit of generosity for a true Christian involvement with the world.

- Parish Missions:
  1. View the parish mission as an opportunity for parish spiritual renewal in the spirit of the primitive Pauline Apostolic visitation.
  2. Preach the basic good news, all of it in true perspective. (St. Paul, not Billy Sunday.)
  3. Prepare for this rare opportunity for parish renewal.

- Retreat:
  - Remember: the retreat is a time of intensification of union with Jesus.
  - It is comprised of three fundamental elements:
    1. Solitude.
    2. Re-establishment.
    3. Jesus.
    ("Come apart into a desert place and rest awhile.")
  - Introduce Jesus to your listeners in a more personal, more intimate way.
  - Re-establish your listeners in a greater commitment to Jesus and to all men.
  - Preach the basic good news at greater length and with greater relevancy to whatever group you are addressing.
  - Take particular care to make your sermons interesting, and do not forget that priceless quality of humor.

CONCLUSION

During the course of this book I have attempted to describe the contemporary preacher. I have tried to indicate his problem, his opportunities, and a method for homiletic development.

My intention was not to be unduly critical of current homiletic efforts, particularly of the long hours of dedicated service that preachers have given to the pulpit. Wherever there have been difficulties, they have been chiefly caused by a faulty homiletic tradition. We are heirs to this tradition of imprecise articulation of the Christian message, a clumsy ecclesiastical jargon, and a lack of enthusiasm for good public speaking. Preaching became one of the many chores the busy priest had to perform in the midst of a crowded and dedicated life, instead of a primary apostolate immediately identified with his priesthood. The real loser, however, in that tradition of diminished enthusiasm for good preaching has been the average Catholic in the pew. A modern layman describes the situation:

> Most of the sermons which I hear give the impression that the priest as a man is not really interested in what he is talking about, that he has never broken through to the thing itself or questioned himself about it or tried to relate it to the rest of his life, or thought about it in the language he would use to discuss other serious human affairs. That man, I feel—if I reflect on the matter at all—has remained content with his verbal formulae.
>
> (Desmond Fennell in *Doctrine and Life*, Oct., 1964)

Statements like that indicate the opportunities which the preacher has lost for communicating the good news, for presenting Jesus, for making Christianity relevant and contemporary, for engaging his listener in an authentic Christian life. The priest is, by vocation, the herald of the good news: he must present the Christian message, as his duty, as his privilege, and as his unique opportunity. Each Sunday Catholics throughout the world listen to thousands of sermons, and the church is thereby presented with a rare opportunity to change men's lives. But that cannot be accomplished if the priest does not preach well. We face the Christian people from the pulpit each Sunday, and whom can we blame but ourselves if their lives remain unchanged?

This book presents a precise program for the development of an effective contemporary preacher. If the preacher studies the argument of this book, reviews the exercises, and practices them, he will become a true, enthusiastic herald of the good news. He needs to master the principles in Part I, The Art of Public Speaking, training himself to become a poised and communicative speaker. He needs to grasp the principles of Part II and compose sermons that are informative, persuasive, and interesting. And he needs to understand the outline of Part III, The Art of Preaching, and become an enthusiastic herald of the good news, preaching the authentic Christian message.

Two final comments about that program:

1. Public speaking is a perfectible art. It admits of growing and increasing proficiency—when there is a program of practice. The more one practices the principles of good public speaking, the better public speaker he will become. Hence, if the reader of this book will practice the exercises that were outlined, he will show a marked and astonishing improvement in his public speaking. Let him review the exercises of good public speaking, the principles of sermon composition, the basic nature of the good news. Five minutes a day for six months. Or better, a year.

Will you try it? It is a small price to pay for such an enormous benefit.

2. The most celebrated and distinguished of public speakers find it necessary, even after years of speaking, to review the principles of oratory. Everyone develops unconscious faults of technique in public speaking, and it is necessary to submit oneself to periodic

reviews of fundamental principles. Accordingly, the reader of this book should, even after he has mastered the basic principles, review them from time to time, re-examine them, and practice the exercises again. It is insurance that he will continue to be a good public speaker.

Practice and review make the enthusiastic herald of the good news. And that is what society needs today: men who will continue what Jesus started—"Jesus came into Galilee, preaching the good news of God's kingdom."

Appendix

The late Ignatius Smith, O.P., for many years director of the Preacher's Institute of America, stated that many fine public speakers came through the Institute but very few good public readers.

That is quite understandable, because public reading is a different and more difficult art than public speaking. In public speaking, the preacher communicates directly with the audience in his own words and with his own ideas. But in public reading, he must use someone else's ideas and someone else's words—a third man has intruded. It is difficult enough sometimes to communicate directly with an audience, but those problems are compounded immeasurably when one must communicate through another's words and ideas. In addition, the public reader must keep his attention on the matter he is reading, and another barrier to audience contact is erected. No wonder there are so few effective public readers.

Yet public reading has become more important for the priest today as the result of the vernacular liturgy, and it is now imperative for him to attempt to master some of the fundamental principles of this art. The American Bishops' Commission of the Liturgical Apostolate stated that there is "the greatest possibility of scandal if in the new English usage in the Mass the prayers and scriptural passages are read hurriedly or without attention."

Without an extensive study of the art of public reading, there are four basic principles that can serve the journeyman reader adequately for his needs:

1. *Study the meaning.* The reader should study his material in advance, reading it carefully to obtain the precise meaning he wants to communicate to his listeners. This is particularly true when the

reader is using new translations of Scripture with which he is unfamiliar.

2. *Pace the material.* All that we have previously said about pace has particular meaning in the art of reading. The reader must pace and phrase his material carefully so that his listeners can understand every word. He normally needs to pace it a little more slowly than in the practice of public speaking.

3. *Project the material.* The reader must communicate with his audience, thus he must employ all our techniques of projection. He must still hit that back wall. The book he is reading from can divert him so much that he loses all contact with the audience. A good technique for the public reader, therefore, is to look up at the audience occasionally during his reading—at the end of sentences, between paragraphs. And if he finds that the physical arrangements of his lectern are making him bend his neck down into the book, then he should hold the book in one hand out in front of him—in this way he will be projecting directly at the audience.

4. *Modulate the material.* The public reader must read with expression, just as the public speaker. He needs to recall all the techniques of modulation and expression so that his reading will be meaningful and natural for the audience. He does not need to dramatize the material, but he needs to read it in the normal cadences of the human voice. Monotone and sing-song are just as disastrous here as in public speaking.

Study the meaning of the material, pace it properly, project it at the audience, and modulate it naturally. These rules are simple and effective, and they should be practiced. They will serve the average reader to communicate the written word with meaning and understanding.